CRISPR

A POWERFUL WAY TO
CHANGE DNA

WRITTEN BY
YOLANDA RIDGE

ILLUSTRATED BY
ALEX BOERSMA

annick press
toronto + berkeley

Cover art by Alex Boersma, designed by Danielle Arbour with Paul Covello
Interior design by Danielle Arbour

Annick Press Ltd.

We acknowledge the support of the Canada Council for the Arts and the Ontario Arts Council, and the participation of the Government of Canada/la participation du gouvernement du Canada for our publishing activities.

 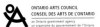

Library and Archives Canada Cataloguing in Publication

Title: CRISPR : a powerful way to change DNA / written by Yolanda Ridge ; illustrated by Alex Boersma.
Names: Ridge, Yolanda, 1973- author. | Boersma, Alex, illustrator.
Identifiers: Canadiana (print) 2020019190X | Canadiana (ebook) 20200191918 | ISBN 9781773214245 (hardcover) | ISBN 9781773214238 (softcover) | ISBN 9781773214276 (PDF) | ISBN 9781773214252 (HTML) | ISBN 9781773214269 (Kindle)
Subjects: LCSH: CRISPR (Genetics)—Juvenile literature. | LCSH: Gene editing—Juvenile literature. | LCSH: Genetics—Juvenile literature. | LCSH: DNA—Juvenile literature.
Classification: LCC QH437.5 .R53 2020 | DDC j576.5—dc23

Published in the U.S.A. by Annick Press (U.S.) Ltd.
Distributed in Canada by University of Toronto Press.
Distributed in the U.S.A. by Publishers Group West.

Printed in Hong Kong

annickpress.com
yolandaridge.com
alexboersma.com

Also available as an e-book. Please visit annickpress.com/ebooks for more details.

This book is dedicated to all my former genetic counseling colleagues, mentors, and friends—and to all of you who will guide society's use of genetic technology into the future. –Y.R.

To my parents, my aunt Karen, and my partner, Nick, for their love and support. –A.B.

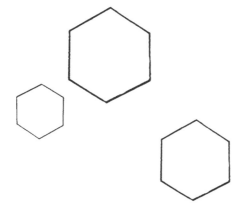

CONTENTS

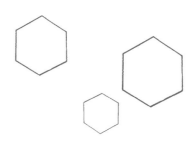

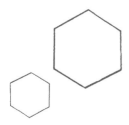

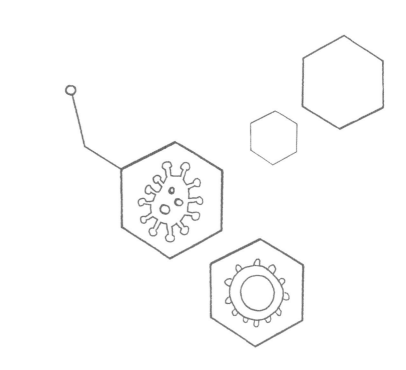

INTRODUCTION

Imagine a world where no one ever gets sick—not even your pet. Imagine there's enough food to feed everyone without destroying the environment. A world where cloned versions of extinct animals are free to roam the earth once again.

Sound too good to be true?

You might be surprised to learn that all of this—and more—could be our new reality thanks to CRISPR, a biotechnology that gives humans the power to edit genes in a way that's never been possible before.

In this book, we'll discuss how gene editing could be used to wipe out disease-carrying mosquitoes and bring back a version of the woolly mammoth. How it could help cure cancer and prevent future pandemics. And how we may be able to create food that can adapt to climate change and be allergy-free and packed full of nutrition. (Chocolate that's even more nutritious than kale? Yes, please!)

Since CRISPR technology is new and constantly evolving, it's hard to predict what life will be like in a gene-edited future. The possilibites are endless and amazing—but they're also a bit scary. Humans haven't done a great job of caring for our planet so far, so what happens when we start messing with the entire web of life? Or altering the natural course of evolution? At what point do we change the definition of what it means to be human?

As we dig into the science behind CRISPR, we'll also explore the pros and cons of gene editing (check out the Stop, Go, and Yield sections at the end of each chapter) and ask some questions to get you thinking about how it might affect your life (see Cutting Questions). In the not-so-distant future, it will be up to each and every one of us to decide whether society should proceed, not proceed, or proceed with caution as we move forward with this powerful technology.

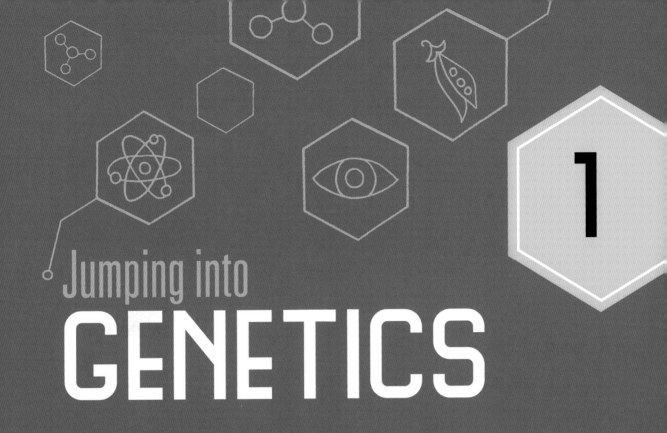

Jumping into
GENETICS

Knowing it's possible to gene-edit our way to better health, better nutrition, and a world without extinctions is one thing, but understanding how is something else altogether. How can we "edit out" a person's chance of inheriting a certain disease, for example, or "edit in" a particular crop's resistance to a certain pest? In order to understand how gene editing works, we first need to understand how genes themselves go about their business.

▮ The Genome: Your Personal Instruction Manual

Let's start with the big picture. Every living being—from a bacteria to a monkey—has a genome. The genome is like a really detailed instruction manual. Not only does it tell the body how to function, but it also makes sure this information gets passed down from generation to generation. It's the instructions in your genome that told your body how to do everything from growing a toe to building a brain (with added information about how to keep it running). The genome gave your parents a similar set of instructions, and it will make sure that any kids you have will know how to do this stuff too.

Since every species is different, the genome of every species is different (although the genome of a mosquito and the genome of an elephant are more similar than you might expect). For now, let's focus on the being that matters to us most—the human being.

Most cells in the human body keep a copy of the entire instruction manual in their command center—otherwise known as the nucleus. It's estimated that the average human body is made up of 37.2 trillion cells— yes, you read that right: 37,200,000,000,000. That's a lot of instruction manuals!

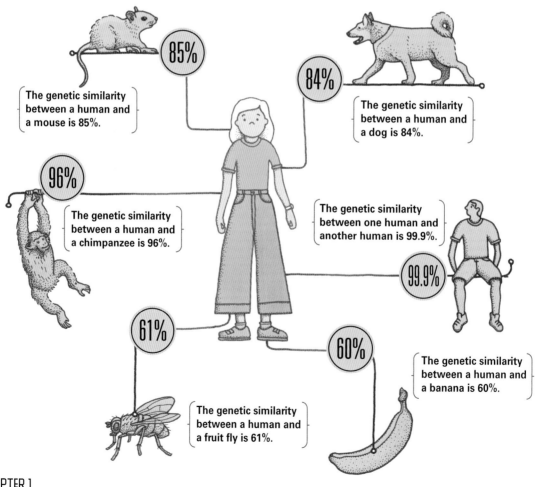

85%

The genetic similarity between a human and a mouse is 85%.

84%

The genetic similarity between a human and a dog is 84%.

96%

The genetic similarity between a human and a chimpanzee is 96%.

99.9%

The genetic similarity between one human and another human is 99.9%.

61%

The genetic similarity between a human and a fruit fly is 61%.

60%

The genetic similarity between a human and a banana is 60%.

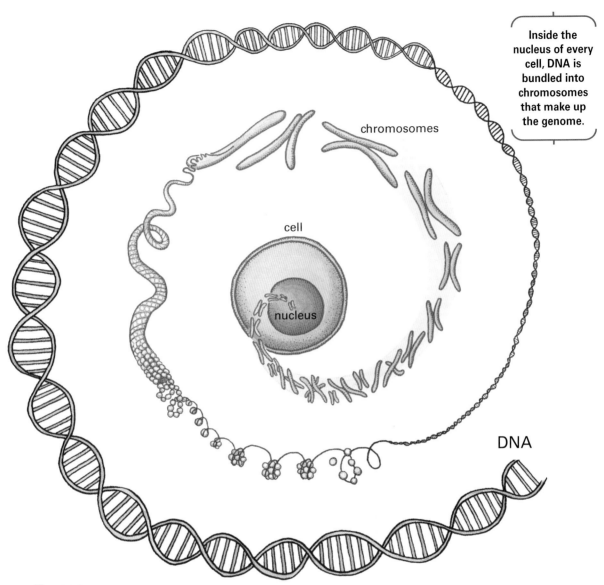

chromosomes

cell

nucleus

DNA

▌DNA

Instead of being written in words, like the instruction manuals we're used to, the genome is written with DNA. If you were to unravel the genome and zoom in with a *really* powerful microscope, you'd eventually see that DNA is the core of it all.

So, what is DNA? The letters stand for "deoxyribonucleic acid," which is a long way of saying that DNA is made up of two long strings of molecules called nucleotides.

These strings—or strands—spiral together to create what's known as a double helix. If you think of DNA as a twisted ladder, each strand of nucleotides is one side of the ladder. The rungs that attach the sides together are formed by the nitrogen base of each nucleotide binding with its mate on the other side. This is why nucleotide pairs are often referred to as "base pairs."

Our alphabet has 26 letters; DNA has 4—A, G, T, and C—which stand for the nucleotides adenine, guanine, thymine, and cytosine. In DNA, adenine pairs with thymine, and cytosine pairs with guanine.

The workers inside the cell read sequences of three nucleotides as three-letter words, or codons. These three-letter words then string together to form a sentence. And these sentences make up the instruction manual.

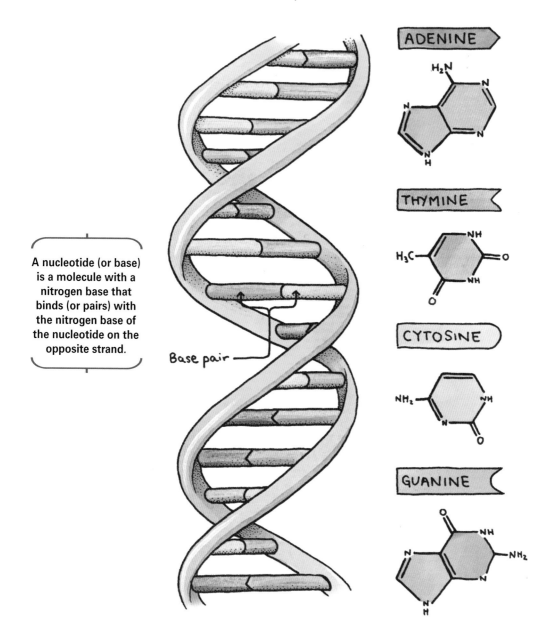

A nucleotide (or base) is a molecule with a nitrogen base that binds (or pairs) with the nitrogen base of the nucleotide on the opposite strand.

Base pair

ADENINE

THYMINE

CYTOSINE

GUANINE

To get a sense of how this works, let's imagine that our genome is an instruction manual on how to build things out of toy bricks.

Of course, the human genome isn't instructing the body on how to build a rainbow. Instead, it's telling our 37 trillion cells how to do everything from thinking to digesting food—all of the essential "instructions" we need to function.

1 We look through the instruction manual to find what we want to build—say, a rainbow.

2 At the beginning of the step-by-step instructions on how to build a rainbow, there will be a three-letter word (or codon) that means START.

3 Right after that will be a three-letter word that tells us which brick to get first.

4 The three-letter word that comes next is the code for the next size and shape of brick you need to add.

5 And so on . . . until you get to a three-letter word that means STOP.

6 Your rainbow is complete!

▌Genes

So, where do genes fit in? If the genome is the cell's entire instruction manual, the gene is like a specific sentence. It tells the cell how to make one specific thing—a protein. When making a protein, the two strands of DNA split apart so they can be copied by something called messenger RNA, or mRNA. (RNA, which stands for "ribonucleic acid," is just a single-stranded version of DNA with U standing in for T.) The three-letter words in the mRNA are then used to build a protein using amino acids. Like the toy bricks used to make our rainbow, amino acids are building blocks made of elements from the periodic table that come together in different combinations to form a protein.

Now, a rainbow's not particularly useful (unless you're into photography or hunting for pots of gold), but proteins are necessary for every single thing our bodies do, from digesting food (using enzymes) to determining traits like eye color (with different pigment proteins) or height (through hormones).

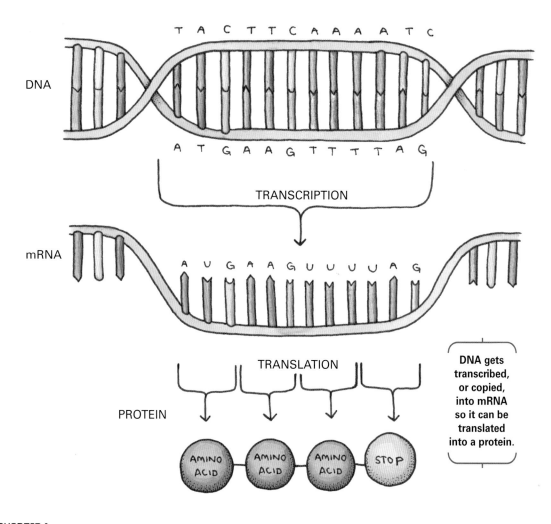

DNA

T A C T T C A A A A T C

A T G A A G T T T T A G

TRANSCRIPTION

mRNA

A U G A A G U U U U A G

TRANSLATION

PROTEIN

AMINO ACID — AMINO ACID — AMINO ACID — STOP

DNA gets transcribed, or copied, into mRNA so it can be translated into a protein.

The Father of Genetics

Gregor Mendel—the "father of genetics"—was an Austrian monk who liked to grow peas. Also a budding scientist, he was curious as to why plants had different traits. To test how things like height, shape, and color were inherited, Mendel made plant "moms" and plant "dads" produce plant "babies" by controlling pollination.

When a tall mama plant crossed with a small papa plant, it did not produce a medium-sized baby plant, as Mendel had predicted. Instead, the baby plant was tall. Over the course of his experiments, Mendel learned that the tall trait was "dominant" over the small trait. What Mendel discovered from these experiments done in the 1850s formed the basis of what we now know about dominant and recessive traits.

Short pea plant
(*tt*)

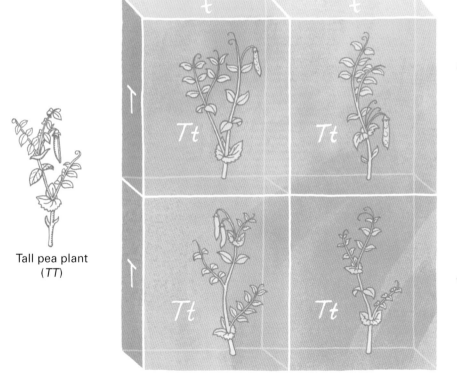

Tall pea plant
(*TT*)

If a tall pea plant has two tall genes (labeled *T*), it can only pass on a *T* to the next generation. If a small pea plant has two small genes (labeled *t*), it can only pass on a *t* to the next generation. Every pea plant in the next generation will be tall since the *T* version of the gene is dominant over *t*.

All baby pea plants are tall.

▌Chromosomes

All of this DNA—the letters that code for genes and the non-coding regions in between them—are bundled into chromosomes. The human genome has 46 chromosomes that are grouped into pairs.

Chromosomes 1 through 22 (the autosomes, conveniently numbered according to size) all have a partner that's similar but not identical. Both copies of chromosome 15, for example, contain a gene for eye color. But one copy of that gene might code for brown eyes and the other for blue eyes—similar but not identical (see "Look into My Eyes," page 12).

The 23rd pair—the sex chromosomes—do not necessarily pair up. Females have two X chromosomes, which are as similar to each other as a pair of autosomes. Males have one X chromosome and one Y chromosome, which are quite different in both size and content. In fact, the Y chromosome only contains genes that code for proteins needed to make male reproductive parts. So, if you get a Y—biologically, you're male.

 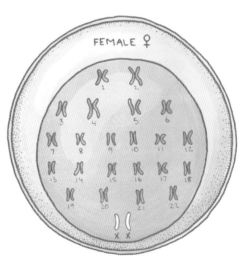

A complete set of human chromosomes after they've been isolated in the nucleus, stained, and magnified

Why do we need two copies of every chromosome? Mainly because of inheritance. Each pair contains one chromosome from our mom and one from our dad.

When a skin cell or a brain cell, for example, divides to make a new cell, it copies every page of the instruction manual—or every chromosome—to produce a clone of itself. But when a reproductive cell divides to make an egg or sperm, it reduces its chromosomes by half. This is why human children are not clones of their parents but rather a combination of the two.

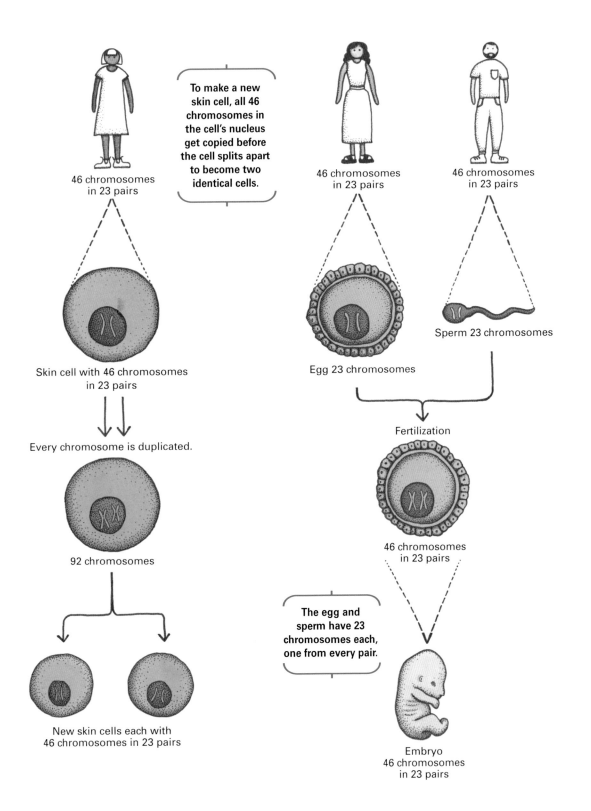

46 chromosomes
in 23 pairs

To make a new skin cell, all 46 chromosomes in the cell's nucleus get copied before the cell splits apart to become two identical cells.

46 chromosomes
in 23 pairs

46 chromosomes
in 23 pairs

Skin cell with 46 chromosomes
in 23 pairs

Egg 23 chromosomes

Sperm 23 chromosomes

Every chromosome is duplicated.

Fertilization

92 chromosomes

46 chromosomes
in 23 pairs

The egg and sperm have 23 chromosomes each, one from every pair.

New skin cells each with
46 chromosomes in 23 pairs

Embryo
46 chromosomes
in 23 pairs

So now we understand why we're half like our mom and half like our dad (although some of us may prefer to think of ourselves as more like one than the other!). We also understand how DNA makes up genes, and genes make up chromosomes, and chromosomes make up our entire genome, which acts like an instruction manual for producing the proteins we need to develop, grow, and function. Now that we've got that figured out, we're ready to explore the amazing technology that is gene editing.

EYE COLOR   MELANUCYTES IN THE IRIS

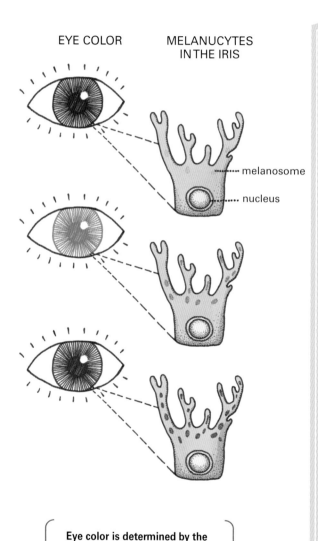

···· melanosome

···· nucleus

Eye color is determined by the amount of pigment produced and stored in the cells within the iris.

Look into My Eyes

When scientists first figured out that genes were responsible for the traits passed on from parents to children, they assumed that simple characteristics like eye color were controlled by a single gene. Just like Gregor Mendel described the "tall" pea plant trait as dominant over the "small" trait (see "The Father of Genetics," page 9), brown eyes were thought to be dominant over blue eyes and green eyes.

Turns out that was too simple an explanation. We now know there are many different genes involved in determining eye color. Some of these genes provide a set of instructions on how much pigment specific cells within the iris should make. In addition to other factors such as the structure of your eye, color is determined by the amount of pigment made and stored in the iris.

Chromosome 15 has two genes that play a big role in this. Since those two genes are close together on the same autosome, they usually get passed on as a pair, which is why two blue-eyed parents are very likely to have blue-eyed children. But if you happen to have brown eyes, even though your parents both have blue eyes, don't assume you were switched at birth. It's just the result of those other genes doing their thing.

Rewriting the
GENOME

Our ability to change and rearrange the genome—or instruction manual—isn't new.

When our early ancestors started domesticating plants (by collecting and planting the seeds of wild wheat) and animals (by taming wild goats), they selected which plants to grow and which animals to keep based on certain qualities. If a wheat stalk grew extra tall and had strong kernels that could survive a windstorm, for example, the seeds from that specific stalk were replanted to grow the next crop. Those farmers might not have recognized it at the time, but they were genetically engineering plants and animals by selecting which specific traits they wanted passed on to the next generation.

These days, products that have been genetically engineered are everywhere—in your closet, at the grocery store, and even in your cereal bowl! If you ate a bowl of cornflakes for breakfast or a salad for lunch, there's a good chance you ate genetically modified food. If you chew sugar-free gum or wear cotton T-shirts, you're in contact with more genetic modification.

A *History of* Genetic Engineering

Humans have engineered living things for thousands of years.
Let's take a look at some significant firsts:

1700s—Selective breeding is recognized as a science, even though civilizations have been using it to strengthen desirable traits in plants and animals for as many as 10,000 years.

1850s—Mendel's experiments with pea plants show how traits are passed on from parent to offspring (see chapter 1).

1996—Dolly the sheep, the first cloned animal, is born.

1994—Flavr Savr tomatoes, the first transgenic food, hit the grocery stores (see chapter 6).

1991—Ashanthi De Silva, a four-year-old girl suffering from an immune disorder, receives the first successful gene therapy.

2003—A tropical fish that fluoresces bright red becomes the first genetically modified pet to go on sale in the United States.

2007—Scientists figure out that CRISPR-Cas9 is part of the bacterial immune system.

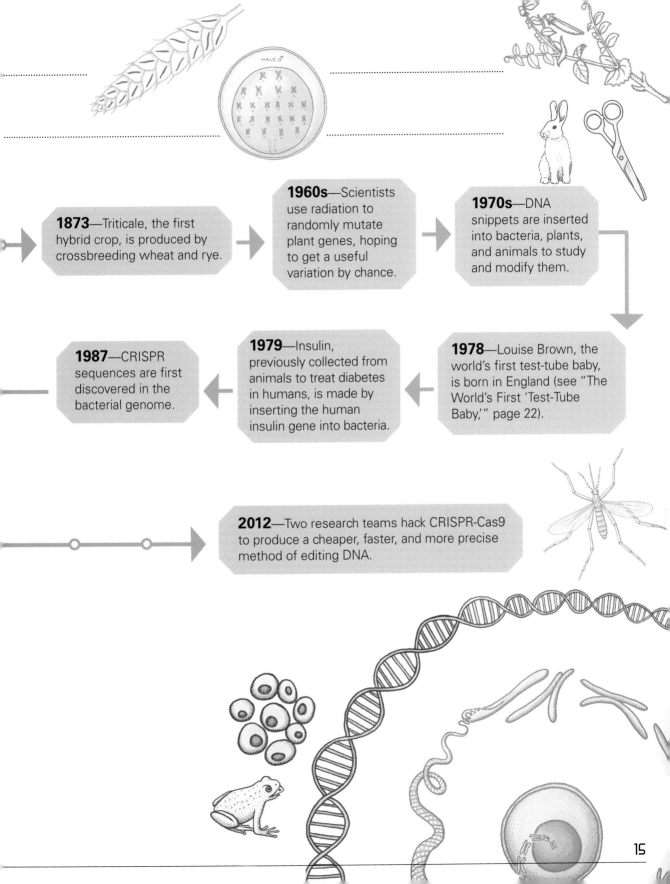

1873—Triticale, the first hybrid crop, is produced by crossbreeding wheat and rye.

1960s—Scientists use radiation to randomly mutate plant genes, hoping to get a useful variation by chance.

1970s—DNA snippets are inserted into bacteria, plants, and animals to study and modify them.

1987—CRISPR sequences are first discovered in the bacterial genome.

1979—Insulin, previously collected from animals to treat diabetes in humans, is made by inserting the human insulin gene into bacteria.

1978—Louise Brown, the world's first test-tube baby, is born in England (see "The World's First 'Test-Tube Baby,'" page 22).

2012—Two research teams hack CRISPR-Cas9 to produce a cheaper, faster, and more precise method of editing DNA.

MALE ♂

▮ Introducing . . . CRISPR

So, if we can already genetically alter everything from food to animals, what's the big deal about CRISPR? Genetic modifications done before the development of CRISPR took a lot of time and a bit of luck and had a whole lot of limitations. With CRISPR, we can now alter a species by editing its genes in much more controlled, specific, and powerful ways.

CRISPR—pronounced "crisper"—stands for Clustered Regularly Interspaced Short Palindromic Repeats. That's quite a mouthful of words we don't commonly use, so let's break it down, starting at the end.

The last three letters of the CRISPR acronym—SPR—describe a specific sequence of DNA.

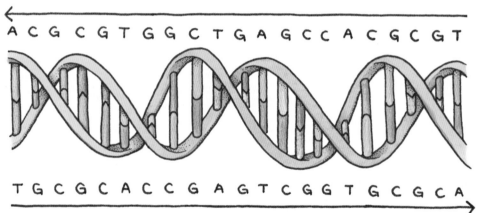

A C G C G T G G C T G A G C C A C G C G T

A "short" sequence of nucleotides

A C G C G T G G C T G A G C C A C G C G T

T G C G C A C C G A G T C G G T G C G C A

In a palindromic sequence, the two strands of DNA are the same when read in opposite directions.

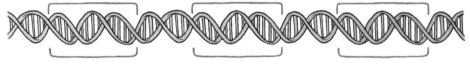

Repeating sequences of DNA clustered together with sections of non-repeating, unique DNA sequences in between.

- Short means the sequence is about 20 to 40 base pairs long.

- Palindromic means those 20 to 40 base pairs can be read the same way backward or forward. In our world, a "palindrome" is a word like KAYAK, in which the letters can be read the same way backward and forward. In the DNA world, it means that the two strands, when read in opposite directions, provide the same set of instructions.

- Repeats mean that identical copies of this sequence are repeated over and over again. (Finally, a word that makes sense!)

Now, back to the beginning of our acronym—CRISPR. The first three letters tell us where these short palindromic repeats are located. Clustered means they're found together in the genome, and Regularly Interspaced refers to the fact that between these repeats are unique pieces of DNA.

Unraveling a Mystery

When scientists first discovered CRISPR in bacteria, they had no idea what these repeating sequences were for. And they were even more confused by the unique pieces of DNA found between them. What were they up to?

Turns out, CRISPR is an important part of the bacteria's immune system. It's used as a way of learning from past infections and preparing for future attacks.

When a bacterial cell successfully fights off a viral invasion (yes, bugs do attack bugs!), it keeps a piece of the attacker's DNA for future reference. This unique piece of DNA gets stored right in the bacteria's own genome.

Remember our instruction manual from chapter 1? Well, these pieces of viral DNA get grouped (or clustered) together in what could be described as troubleshooting sections—the parts of the instruction manual that describe what to do when something goes wrong. And to make extra sure that the bacteria doesn't get confused and start accidentally making proteins from these bits of viral DNA, the troubleshooting sections are all clearly marked by CRISPR's short palindromic repeats.

The next time the bacteria senses an attack, it searches the troubleshooting sections of its genome to try to identify the attacker. If the attacker's DNA matches any DNA sequence stored between those short palindromic repeats, the bacterial cell learns from the past infection and destroys the invader.

Cas9: The Power behind CRISPR

How exactly does the bacteria destroy the invading virus? This is where the workers of the cell—the proteins—come into the picture. Even though CRISPR gets all the fame, the hard work is actually done by CRISPR-associated proteins, or Cas proteins. These proteins are made by cas genes, which are conveniently located right next door to CRISPR in the genome.

Some of the cas genes make proteins that work like a zipper to unwind DNA. They're called helicases. Other cas genes make proteins that work like scissors to cut DNA. They're called nucleases.

cas genes

CRISPR

The Cas proteins are made from genes located next to the CRISPR repeats.

These proteins join together to form Cas complexes. There are several different types of Cas complexes, but we'll stick with Cas9 since it was the first one adapted for human purposes. In theory, this system could be used in any type of cell, but in nature, CRISPR's only found in bacteria and other simple, single-celled organisms.

When a bacterial cell senses an invasion, Cas9 takes a photocopy of all the unique DNA sequences stored in CRISPR from previous attacks. With a copy of the sequence—known as guide RNA (gRNA)—Cas9 gets to work, searching the genome of the invader for a match. It's a bit like an antivirus software program on your computer searching its files for signature sequences.

If Cas9 finds the matching sequence, it knows the invader is a virus (and not just any virus—the relative of a previous attacker). The helicase part of the protein complex unwinds the double helix of the virus's DNA. Then the nuclease snips the DNA apart. Now the virus can't infect the bacteria; once its DNA's been cut up, it's as good as gone.

Not a bad defense system for a simple bacterial cell, right? But here's what makes it even better. Because the bacteria has incorporated the viral DNA into its own genome, it can now pass the information down to future generations. When the bacteria divides, all of its DNA gets copied— including whatever viral sequences have been stored in those CRISPRs.

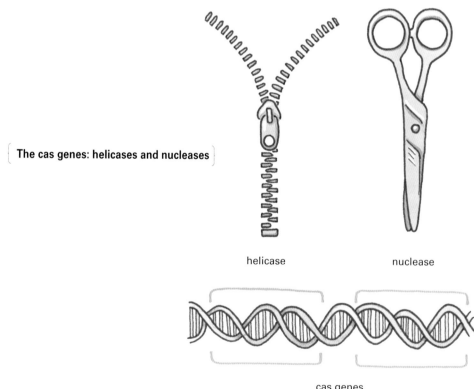

The cas genes: helicases and nucleases

helicase

nuclease

cas genes

The CRISPR-Cas9 Process

Step 1: Unique pieces of DNA stored between repeats are copied into gRNA.

Step 2: Cas9 carries the gRNA through the virus's genome, searching for matching DNA sequences.

Step 3: When Cas9 finds a matching sequence, the helicase separates the DNA strands.

Step 4: The Cas9 nuclease snips the DNA.

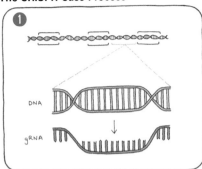

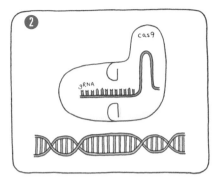

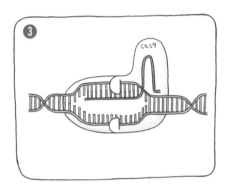

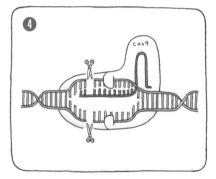

▮ Hacking the System

So, why is everyone so excited about the defense system of a simple bacterial cell? Because scientists have figured out how to hack the CRISPR system so it can be used to edit the DNA of any given species.

With a little programming, CRISPR-Cas9 can be made to function like the find-and-cut or even the find-and-replace mechanism in your word processing program. Here's how it works:

❶ Scientists attach a specific 20-letter sequence of guide RNA to Cas9. (This guide RNA can be built in a lab by copying a target sequence from whatever species they're working with.)

❷ Using this guide RNA, Cas9 searches through the entire genome of whatever cell it's delivered to, looking for a match (see chapter 5 for more on how Cas9 is delivered to the cell).

❸ When Cas9 finds a DNA sequence that matches the guide RNA, it starts snipping.

Unlike for the poor virus in the bacterial defense system, this is not where the story ends. When the specific DNA sequence gets cut, the targeted cell immediately goes to work to repair the damage. There are two ways this can happen.

▌Find and Cut

This method is as simple as it sounds—as easy, in fact, as removing an unwanted word from a sentence in your English essay. Once Cas9 cuts the DNA, the cell glues the strands back together. In this process, a few base pairs are usually lost. This might not seem like a big deal, but if the guide RNA directs Cas9 to the coding region of a gene, it's enough to mess up the three-letter code we talked about in chapter 1. This is how CRISPR-Cas9 is used to "knock out" a gene: the changes are enough to make sure that the instructions no longer code for a functional protein.

Here's what that might look like using our familiar 26-letter alphabet. Before CRISPR-Cas9, this section of DNA—THECATSATONAMAT—would be read in three-letter words by the cell as THE CAT SAT ONA MAT. (Okay, ONA isn't exactly a word, but it's still easy to figure out what the sentence means.) If we send in Cas9 with a guide RNA for THECATSATONAMAT, the nuclease might cut it here:

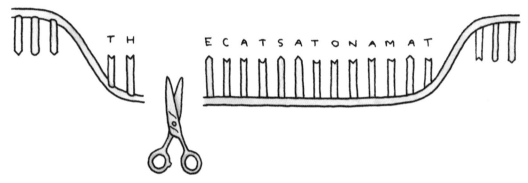

Next, the cell will glue the rest of the "sentence" back together. But it won't be able to include the base pairs right next to the cut because they've been damaged by the nuclease.

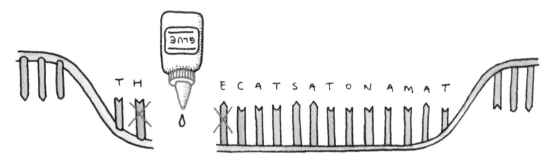

Now the cell will read this repaired sequence as TCA TSA TON AMA T . . . a sentence (or gene) that makes no sense (or protein) at all! This set of instructions would be ignored by the cell in the same way we skip the pages of an instruction manual written in a language we don't understand.

▌Find and Replace

In addition to cutting a specific DNA sequence, the cell can also replace it with something else. To make this happen, scientists must supply Cas9 with a template of the DNA it wants inserted at the site of the break. The cell will then use this template to rebuild the DNA during the repair process.

The sentence THE CAT SAT ONA MAT is replaced by THE OLD DOG SAT AND ATE. In the same way, find and replace deletes one gene and replaces it with another. If we pretend our genome contains a set of instructions on how to make a rainbow like we did in chapter 1, this would be like taking out that set of instructions and replacing it with instructions on how to make a house instead. It could also be used to edit the instructions so that the blue stripe in the rainbow is now black (or brown or whatever color the scientist prefers!).

What Exactly Is Genetic Engineering?

This question is harder to answer than it should be because terms like "engineered," "altered," and "modified" often get used interchangeably. To make things even more confusing, definitions also vary between dictionaries and science books. Here are some generally accepted meanings to get us on the same page (no pun intended):

"Genetic engineering" is the manipulation of an organism's genome by human technology. It can refer to anything from selective breeding to the direct alteration of an organism's DNA.

"Transgenic" refers to an organism that's had a gene from another organism inserted into its genome. It is often called a "genetically modified organism," or GMO. The Flavr Savr tomato, for example, has a gene added to its genome to slow down the rotting process (see chapter 6 for more on this).

CRISPR technology is very specifically referred to as gene editing because the changes it makes to DNA are so precise and accurate.

To truly use CRISPR to our advantage, we must first know which gene we want to target. And that requires knowing what a specific gene does within a specific species. Once we know the gene, we must also know the sequence. Only then can we send Cas9 into a cell to knock out the gene—or use the find-and-replace feature to insert a sequence of nucleotides into a specific spot in the genome.

Before CRISPR, genetic engineering was a bit like opening an instruction manual to a random page and stuffing in a bunch of extra letters. Other gene-editing enzymes, such as "zinc finger nucleases" and "transcription activator-like effector nucleases" (or ZFN and TALEN—because scientists sure do love their acronyms!), can be used to insert bits of information into some areas of the genome but not everywhere. With CRISPR-Cas9, scientists can get rid of a specific set of instructions or insert new information exactly where they want it.

That ability to be super-specific is a game changer. It's taken us from the hit-or-miss approach of a farmer trying to grow better crops or raise stronger cattle to a world in which we can imagine wiping out certain diseases or saving a species from extinction. But it's not as simple as saying full steam ahead. The detailed science behind CRISPR is still being figured out in many different labs around the world. And just because we can do something doesn't mean we should.

In the rest of this book, we'll take a closer look at the ways in which CRISPR might be applied to our world, and consider the effects—both good and bad—that it might have.

The World's First "Test-Tube Baby"

Louise Brown's chromosomes came together in the lab rather than in the bedroom. For nine years, her parents tried to achieve a pregnancy "the old-fashioned way," but because her mom's fallopian tubes were blocked (meaning that the eggs made in her ovaries couldn't travel into her uterus to be fertilized), they weren't successful. That's when the scientists got involved. They surgically removed eggs from the ovary and fertilized them in a petri dish with sperm from Louise's dad. After two days in the petri dish, the resulting embryo was transplanted into Louise's mom's uterus. ("Test-tube baby" must've sounded better than "petri-dish baby.")

Louise's birth was described as a miracle by the press, but it was also very controversial at the time. As with gene editing today, people were concerned about the "slippery slope" of genetic manipulation and the treatment of embryos. Now referred to as IVF, for "in vitro fertilization" ("in vitro," which literally means "in glass," usually refers to something that happens outside the body), the procedure has produced over 5 million babies since Louise was born in 1978.

Better
BLOOD

Here's what we've learned so far: Genes are responsible for the many traits that make us who we are—from eye color and height to our chances of getting certain diseases. CRISPR is a technology that allows us to very specifically edit our genes in ways that can make us (or any other living thing) stronger or healthier or better suited to a particular environment. Scientists are already imagining how to put this amazing tool to work. One thing CRISPR might be able to do is help people with disorders caused by a single-gene mutation.

▋Mucking Around with Mutations

We have *a lot* of genes. Remember the 46 human chromosomes we talked about in chapter 1? Well, there are approximately 3 billion base pairs of DNA bundled up in those chromosomes. If written out using letters the same size as the ones you are reading right now, the "sentence" made by those base pairs would stretch the full length of the border between Canada and the United States. And within that coding DNA, there are around 20,000 different genes.

Every time our genome is copied—which happens every time a new cell is created—mistakes are made. (Who wouldn't make a few errors copying an instruction manual that long?) Some of these mistakes—or mutations—result in small changes, like the gene that produces brown eye pigment becoming a gene for blue eye pigment. Other mistakes are big enough to allow a water-dwelling species to live on land. Ancient fish, for example, were able to make the transition from water to land over 350 million years ago, partly thanks to gene mutations that made their eyes bigger and less round so they could see better in the air.

It's like a recipe being copied from one generation to the next. Grandma makes her famous cookies with cinnamon. Mom reads the instructions wrong and adds cloves instead, making a cookie that's different but equally delicious. When Billy gets a turn, he adds an extra egg (or two). This results in something more like a muffin than a cookie, but it's still a satisfying snack. But if Kimora really reads the recipe wrong and doesn't add flour? She probably won't end up with anything edible at all.

Mutations that change a gene so it no longer produces a working protein can be catastrophic enough to stop life completely. Others can lead to human disorders that scientists have been studying for years.

A stem cell is a unique type of cell that hasn't yet decided what it wants to be when it grows up (partly because it has over 200 different types of cells to choose from!). As an embryonic stem cell gets older, it has fewer options depending on where it ends up. Adult stem cells are found in many parts of the body including the brain, heart, gut, liver, bones, skin, and teeth.

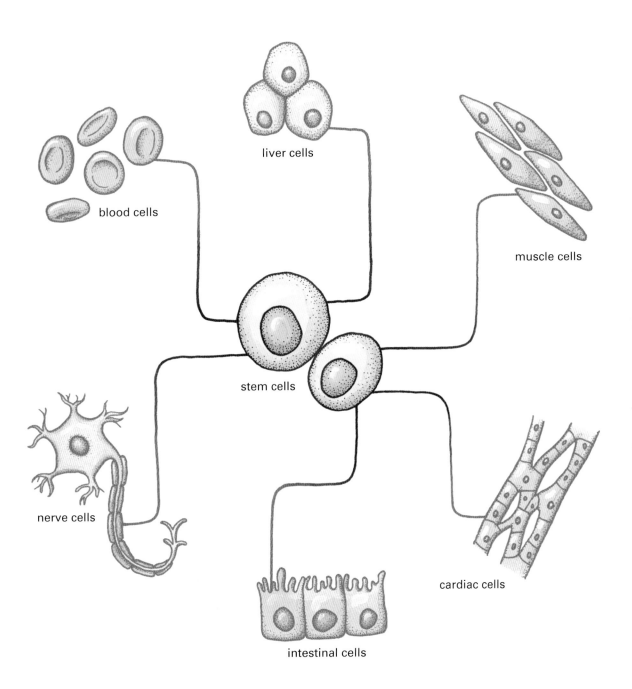

blood cells

liver cells

muscle cells

stem cells

nerve cells

intestinal cells

cardiac cells

▌Sickle Cell Anemia

Sickle cell anemia is a disease caused by a mutation in a single gene. It was discovered in 1910 when a person with joint and stomach pain was found to have oddly shaped red blood cells. To figure out what was going on, scientists worked backward to where the red blood cells were coming from—a type of cell called a stem cell. When a stem cell decides to become a red blood cell, it follows instructions provided by a group of hemoglobin genes. These genes tell the cell how to make the hemoglobin proteins needed to transport oxygen around the body.

A normal red blood cell and a sickle cell

normal red
blood cell

sickle cell

That process works well as long as the instructions are reproduced exactly. But a single spelling mistake—a T where an A is supposed to be—in one of the three-letter words of the hemoglobin gene on chromosome 11 leads to the production of red blood cells that are shaped like a sickle (a semicircular blade) instead of a disk.

Unfortunately, the hemoglobin in this type of red blood cell doesn't transport oxygen very well. And since the sickle shape's not as aerodynamic as the disk shape of a normal red blood cell, sickle-shaped cells can also get stuck inside blood vessels.

Sickle cell anemia is inherited as an autosomal recessive condition (see "How's It Inherited?," page 28). People who inherit one copy of the mutated hemoglobin gene are carriers of what's known as sickle cell trait. Having sickle cell trait comes with advantages (see "Sickle Cell Trait," page 27) and disadvantages, but it doesn't create the medical problems associated with sickle cell anemia. The non-mutated copy of the gene produces enough disk-shaped cells to carry oxygen, and there aren't enough sickle-shaped cells to significantly damage the blood vessels.

But the child of two carriers can inherit two copies of the mutated gene, and no copies of the non-mutated gene. This person—let's call her Anya—will be affected with sickle cell anemia. Since Anya has no disk-shaped red blood cells to transport oxygen, she'll develop anemia—a condition that makes you constantly tired—in early childhood. And as she gets older, those sickle-shaped red blood cells will get hung up inside her blood vessels, blocking blood flow like a stalled car in single-lane traffic, causing Anya severe pain.

There are medications and lifestyle choices that can help people like Anya. But there's no cure for sickle cell anemia. As an adult, she will be at high risk for organ damage, heart failure, and stroke. It's very likely that the disease will shorten her life span.

Sickle Cell Trait

Sickle cell trait—being a carrier of one copy of the mutated hemoglobin gene on chromosome 11—is very common in parts of Africa and South Asia. Interestingly, maps show us that the regions where a lot of people have sickle cell trait are the same regions with a high risk of malaria (an infectious disease we'll talk about in chapter 4).

What's the connection? It might look like what's causing sickle cell trait is also causing malaria, but it's actually the other way around: having sickle cell trait protects a person from developing malaria.

While no one is quite sure how or why someone with sickle cell trait is protected from malaria, we do know that the connection between the two conditions is an example of natural selection—the process of adapting to your environment.

Here's how it works: If you have sickle cell trait, you have an advantage— you won't die of malaria. This means you're more likely to have children than someone who does not have sickle cell trait. And since sickle cell anemia is an autosomal recessive condition—meaning both parents have to have the trait in order to pass it on (see "How's It Inherited?," page 28)—two carriers of sickle cell trait can produce the following:

- a child with two mutated copies of the hemoglobin gene (who will most likely die of sickle cell anemia before they have children of their own)
- a child with two non-mutated copies of the hemoglobin gene (who has a higher risk of developing malaria and dying before they have children of their own)
- a child who also has sickle cell trait (who is the most likely to have children of their own because they do not have sickle cell anemia and are protected from malaria)

As this cycle continues, you can see why future generations would have more and more sickle cell trait. Children with sickle cell trait would grow up, marry, and have children of their own. Even if they partner with someone who does not have the trait, on average half of their children would inherit the trait and be protected from malaria. As long as there is a risk of malaria, people with sickle cell trait will have an advantage over those who do not.

How's It Inherited?

The terms "autosomal recessive" and "autosomal dominant" both refer to conditions associated with the genes on chromosomes 1 to 22 (the autosomes—the chromosomes that are not sex chromosomes).

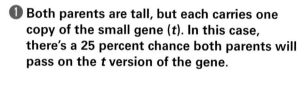

If a trait is autosomal recessive, you need two copies of the gene in order to develop the trait. It's like the small pea plants in Mendel's experiments: they had to inherit two copies of the small gene in order to be small (see "The Father of Genetics," page 9). This can happen in three ways:

❶ **Both parents are tall, but each carries one copy of the small gene (*t*). In this case, there's a 25 percent chance both parents will pass on the *t* version of the gene.**

....

❷ **Both parents are small, which means both carry two copies of the *t* gene. Here, there's a 100 percent chance of the child being small because each small parent will always pass on a copy of the *t* gene.**

....

❸ **One parent is small (*tt*), and one parent is tall but carries one copy of the small gene (*Tt*). Since the small parent can only pass on the small gene, it's all up to the tall parent—and there's a 50 percent chance they'll pass on the small gene and have a small child with this partner.**

If a trait is autosomal dominant, you only need to inherit one copy of the gene to exhibit the trait. In other words, it behaves like the tall pea plant gene. Tall is dominant over small (and small is recessive to tall). This means the child is more likely to be tall than small. Here are the possibilities:

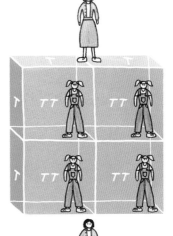

❶ Both parents have two tall (T) genes. In this case, there's a 100 percent chance the child will be tall.

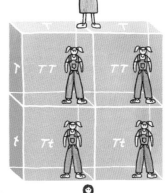

❷ One tall parent has two tall genes (TT) and one tall parent has one tall gene (Tt). Again, there's a 100 percent chance this child will be tall (remember, T is dominant over t, which means that even if the child inherits a t gene, the T will dominate).

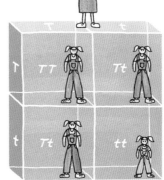

❸ Both parents are tall and both have one copy of the small gene (Tt). This is the opposite of the first scenario we talked about with the autosomal recessive traits (see page 28). In this case, 75 percent of these children will be tall.

If Anya has access to high-quality health care, she may be a candidate for a stem cell transplant. In this procedure, stem cells from a donor who doesn't have sickle cell anemia are transplanted into Anya's blood or bone marrow (the blood-cell-making factory inside our bones). If the transplant works, these new stem cells will become responsible for making new red blood cells using the donor's non-mutated genetic code.

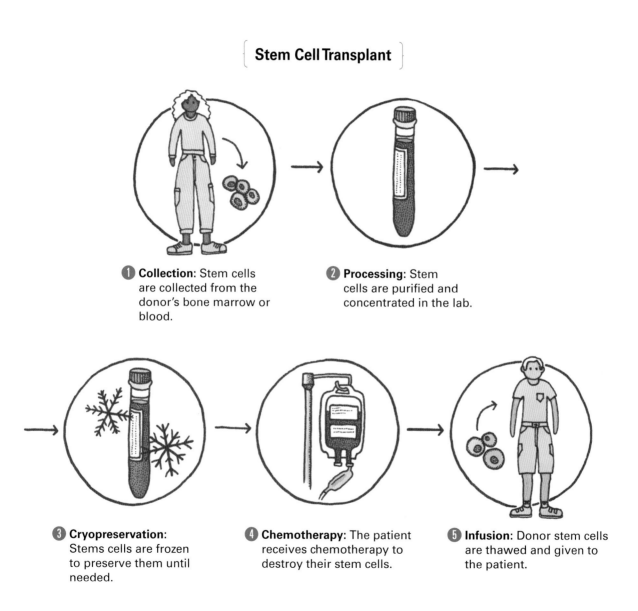

Stem Cell Transplant

1 **Collection:** Stem cells are collected from the donor's bone marrow or blood.

2 **Processing:** Stem cells are purified and concentrated in the lab.

3 **Cryopreservation:** Stems cells are frozen to preserve them until needed.

4 **Chemotherapy:** The patient receives chemotherapy to destroy their stem cells.

5 **Infusion:** Donor stem cells are thawed and given to the patient.

While this sounds like a perfect solution, a stem cell transplant comes with its own risks. The main problem with this treatment goes back to our trusty immune system. Even if the donor is Anya's sister or brother, her immune system will recognize the foreign stem cells as invaders and reject them. To stop this from happening, Anya's immune system must be "turned off" by strong medication that will leave her very vulnerable to other types of infections.

This is where CRISPR comes in. What if Anya's stem cells could be genetically edited? Scientists could give Cas9 a copy of the mutated hemoglobin gene sequence and create a DNA template of the non-mutated code. Instead of using stem cells from a donor, scientists could remove Anya's own stem cells and add this Cas9 mixture to them during step 2. Cas9 would then get to work cutting out the mutated gene sequence and replacing it with the non-mutated code.

Once complete, the CRISPR-modified stem cells would be returned to Anya. Her immune system would welcome them back like long-lost friends. Over time, they would multiply to produce more stem cells, which would eventually become red blood cells. And because these new stem cells contain non-mutated copies of the hemoglobin gene, future red blood cells would be disk-shaped. Anya's sickle cell anemia would essentially be cured.

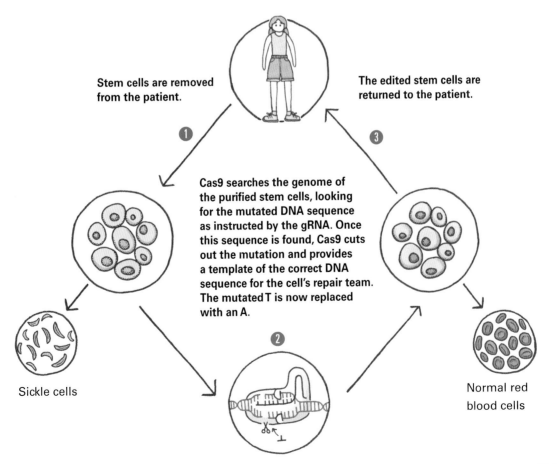

Stem cells are removed from the patient.

The edited stem cells are returned to the patient.

❶

❸

Cas9 searches the genome of the purified stem cells, looking for the mutated DNA sequence as instructed by the gRNA. Once this sequence is found, Cas9 cuts out the mutation and provides a template of the correct DNA sequence for the cell's repair team. The mutated T is now replaced with an A.

❷

Sickle cells

Normal red blood cells

Pass It On

Most of the cells in our body are somatic, meaning that they will not be passed on to the next generation. If a mutation occurs in a somatic cell, it's unlikely to affect the entire body or that person's sexual reproduction. And if a somatic cell is genetically edited, the change will only be present in clones of those cells produced by cell division.

But germline cells (or germ cells)—namely, the sperm or egg—can be inherited by the next generation. Since the cells that make the sperm and the egg also influence the next generation, they're referred to as germline cells as well. And embryonic stem cells—the cells in early embryos that have not yet decided what they will be when they grow up—are also part of the germline because they may grow up to be egg- or sperm-forming cells.

If a mutation occurs in any of these germline cells, or an edit is made, this difference can be inherited by that person's children. And that person's children can pass it on to their children, and so on and so on and so on . . .

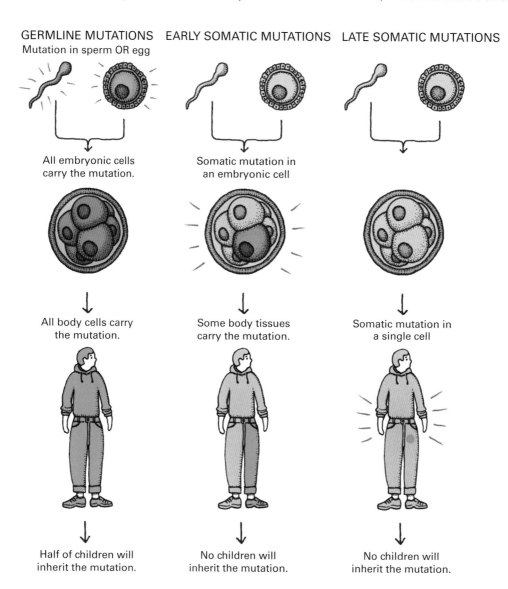

GERMLINE MUTATIONS
Mutation in sperm OR egg

All embryonic cells carry the mutation.

All body cells carry the mutation.

Half of children will inherit the mutation.

EARLY SOMATIC MUTATIONS

Somatic mutation in an embryonic cell

Some body tissues carry the mutation.

No children will inherit the mutation.

LATE SOMATIC MUTATIONS

Somatic mutation in a single cell

No children will inherit the mutation.

Scientists are working hard to make CRISPR treatment for sickle cell anemia an option for those affected.

It's been used to successfully edit the hemoglobin gene in mice. And sickle cell anemia was one of the first inherited conditions to be approved for treatment in human clinical trials.

But there are still details that need to be figured out before this application of CRISPR can be considered safe for individuals like Anya.

• **Detail #1:** Remember that Cas9 is looking for a 20-letter sequence in a 3-billion-letter code. That's kind of like searching for a specific twig somewhere along the Canada–United States border. The Cas9 enzymes can occasionally make a mistake and cut DNA in places that don't match the guide RNA. In human cells, this type of off-target editing could lead to cancer or create other new diseases.

• **Detail #2:** Even if Cas9 does find and cut the code correctly, it's still possible for something to go wrong during the repair stage. In someone with sickle cell anemia, it's important that Cas9 not use the find-and-cut method of fixing DNA damage. As we saw in chapter 2, simply pasting cut DNA back together can create an unreadable set of instructions for the gene (see page 20). In Anya's case, this could mean that her hemoglobin genes don't produce any hemoglobin at all—a condition known as beta thalassemia. Scientists have to be sure that the cell will use the find-and-replace repair mechanism and follow the instructions in Cas9's template.

STOP

Even if CRISPR therapy is possible, there are limits on how it should be used.

Treating sickle cell anemia with CRISPR-edited stem cells is still invasive. Anya wouldn't have to take medicine to suppress her immune system, but she would need chemotherapy to destroy mutated stem cells within the bone marrow so the edited ones can take over.

So, what if we use CRISPR to treat sickle cell anemia at an earlier stage? Instead of waiting until Anya's stem cells have grown up into different cell types, we could modify the mutated DNA in the first two weeks after conception, when Anya's still an embryo. It could also be used before she's conceived—by applying CRISPR to her parents' eggs and sperm or the cells that produce them.

The idea of editing genes in human embryos—or future embryos—raises great social and ethical concerns. Human germline engineering—making changes to the genome that will be passed on to future generations (see "Pass It On," page 32)—is currently banned in many developed countries and highly regulated in others. And research involving human embryonic stem cells is especially controversial.

For the most part, opposition to germline engineering isn't really about the treatment of a disease like sickle cell anemia. But thinking about how it might be used for people like Anya raises questions. If CRISPR technology is perfected for treatment of inherited conditions that are universally accepted as a "disease," how do we stop it from being used for things that do not necessarily lead to human suffering or require medical intervention? Who decides what's a "disease" and what's a "difference"?

We will talk about this more in chapter 9. For now, it's important to know that many people are so concerned about this slippery ethical slope that they don't believe CRISPR should be applied to any human cell therapy at all.

For the 300,000 people born with sickle cell anemia, CRISPR gene therapy could be a life-saver.

The disease is especially common in parts of Africa, where as many as 1 in every 50 individuals is affected by the disease. It may, in fact, be unethical not to pursue further research that could help people like Anya.

Figuring out how to treat sickle cell anemia with CRISPR could also lead to a cure for other inherited diseases. Scientists have focused on sickle cell anemia in part because the gene mutation that causes the disease is very well understood. And since a mutation in a hemoglobin gene only affects the blood, it's possible to target the gene-editing system at specific cells.

If we can get the system to work, the knowledge could be applied to other single-gene diseases, such as:

- **Duchenne muscular dystrophy:** This condition is caused by a mutation in the *DMD* gene on the X chromosome. Affecting mainly boys, it causes muscle degeneration starting at the age of four. Most people with this disease eventually need to use a wheelchair. Because the mutation also affects heart and lung muscles, people with Duchenne muscular dystrophy don't usually live past their 20s.

- **Huntington's disease:** Caused by a mutation in the *HTT* gene on chromosome 4, Huntington's disease is what's known as an autosomal dominant condition (see "How's It Inherited?," page 28). If a person inherits a mutation in just one copy of the gene, they will begin to have uncontrolled jerking or twitching movements in their late 30s or 40s. This will eventually lead to difficulty walking, speaking, and swallowing. This progressive brain disorder also causes emotional problems and loss of thinking ability.

- **Cystic fibrosis:** Like sickle cell anemia, cystic fibrosis is autosomal recessive. To be affected, a person must inherit two mutated copies of the *CFTR* gene on chromosome 7. Without the protein made by *CFTR*, mucus that's supposed to be thin and wet so it can lubricate the organs ends up thick and sticky instead. This usually has the greatest effect on the lungs and pancreas, leading to breathing and digestion problems.

Gene therapy using CRISPR-Cas9 is being studied in animal models of other single-gene disorders as well. With the right checks and balances in place, CRISPR could relieve the suffering of many people affected by serious health problems.

CUTTING QUESTIONS

DISEASE OR DIFFERENCE?

Back in the days of the cave people, being nearsighted was not a disease or a difference—it was deadly. Without glasses, there was no way for our sight-challenged prehistoric ancestors to hunt and care for themselves. They were more likely to end up on another animal's dinner plate than to go to bed with a full belly.

Nearsightedness—also known as myopia—is no longer deadly. But for those of us who can't see anything beyond our own outstretched hands, it's still pretty annoying. Millions of dollars are spent (and made) every year on glasses, contacts, and laser surgery to correct the condition.

Some people might consider myopia a disease since it causes suffering and requires treatment. Other people might consider it a difference since it can be treated and does not reduce a person's life span.

What do you think? If CRISPR could be used to correct someone's eyesight, would it be considered curing a disease or changing a difference?

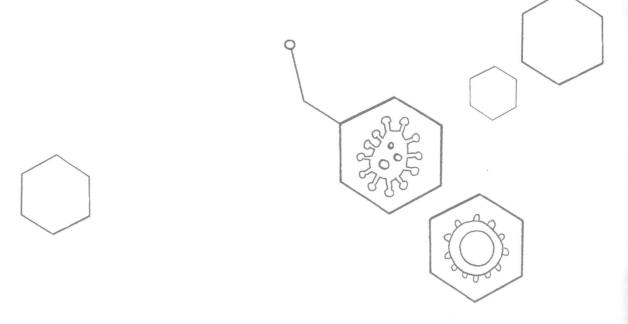

Mutant
MOSQUITOES

In chapter 3, we talked about how sickle cell trait can help protect against malaria, but it's possible that CRISPR can lend a helping hand as well. Malaria is a serious disease caused by a parasite that invades the red blood cells. These parasites—microscopic bugs that get all their nutrients by stealing them from another living organism—make a home for themselves in the blood of either a human or an animal.

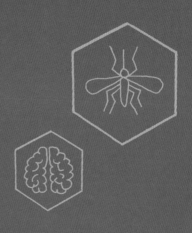

If a human gets infected with such a parasite, they will develop a fever. And as the parasite starts reproducing, it spreads from the liver to the blood where it causes a number of serious health problems. No wonder the World Health Organization (WHO) and others are concerned about the spread of this disease.

▋ Malaria Mayhem

If you've traveled to parts of Africa or South Asia, you've probably taken medication to protect yourself from malaria. While this may keep tourists safe, 1,000 people still die from malaria every single day—mainly children under five years of age living in countries like Uganda, Ghana, and the Democratic Republic of the Congo.

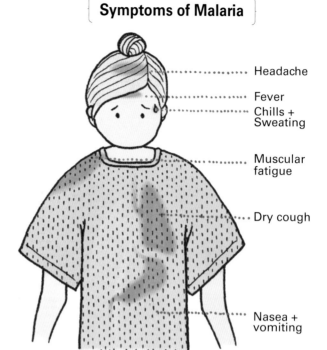

Symptoms of Malaria

- Headache
- Fever
- Chills + Sweating
- Muscular fatigue
- Dry cough
- Nasea + vomiting

Bugs in Burkina Faso

A landlocked country in West Africa is home to an insectary where bugs are kept in secure metal cages under lock and key. Their guards have good reason to be careful—it's hard to keep something contained when it can escape through a hole the size of a pinhead.

What are these scientists so intent on keeping contained? A sterile strain of male mosquitoes developed through gene editing in England and transported to Africa from labs in Italy.

The insectary in Burkina Faso is where many people hope the next step will be made in the fight against malaria. In captivity, the gene-edited male mosquitoes have already mated with local female mosquitoes. As predicted, no offspring were produced. Now the research team hopes to release a small number of sterile males—somewhere in the order of 10,000—to see what happens.

Malaria Around the World

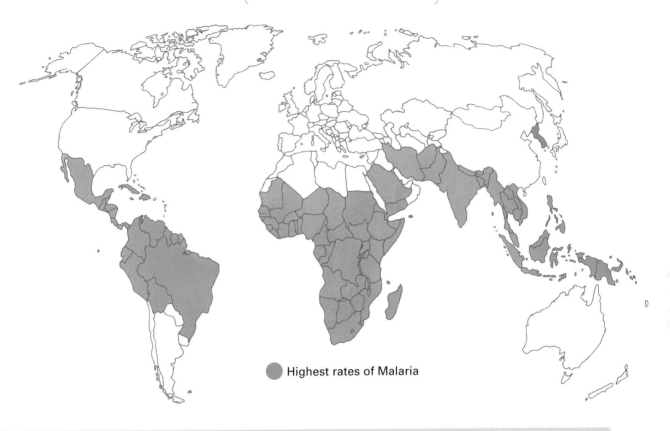

Highest rates of Malaria

These mosquitoes have not been edited to resist malaria. They do not contain gene drives. But they're being used to test the response to genetically edited mosquitoes: from local mosquito populations, from the people of Burkina Faso, and from the global community.

The plan has been approved by the government of Burkina Faso. The research team hopes a successful release will help improve the perception of gene-edited mosquitoes and build trust in the science among regulators and locals. But many local farmers and activists remain opposed.

The United Nations Convention on Biological Diversity has set strict conditions for the eventual release of gene-drive organisms. These conditions include "free, prior and informed consent" of any indigenous communities that could be affected. Whether that's possible—in Burkina Faso or elsewhere in the world—remains to be seen.

Mosquitoes don't cause malaria—that credit goes to the pesky parasite—but they do spread the disease. **Here's how it happens:**

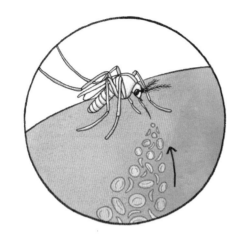

1 A female mosquito bites someone affected with malaria. (Yes—girls only! Male mosquitoes would rather drink flower nectar than human blood.)

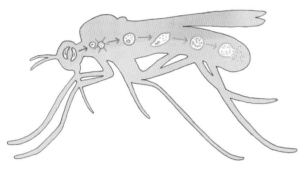

2 The parasite enters the mosquito's body through her victim's blood. And once inside its cozy new home, the parasite grows and multiplies.

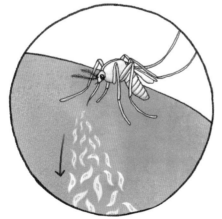

3 The next time that mosquito bites someone, she passes the parasite on.

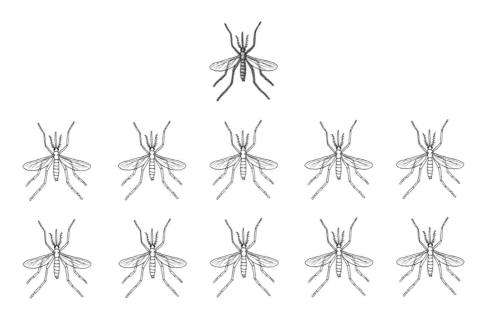

Caused by parasites . . . transmitted by mosquitoes . . . so, what does malaria have to do with genes? Here's a surprising fact: the parasite that causes malaria can't survive in the mosquito's gut without help from a specific protein. And—you guessed it—this protein is made from instructions encoded in a mosquito gene called *FREP1*.

In the same way that CRISPR can fix single-gene mutations like sickle cell anemia, it can create them as well. This has led researchers to wonder whether gene editing could be used to mutate or knock out the *FREP1* gene in mosquitoes so they can no longer transmit malaria. Send in Cas9 with guide RNA of the *FREP1* gene sequence and no repair template, and let it chop away at the DNA. Simple, right?

Sure, that part is simple enough. You can knock out the *FREP1* gene in a single mosquito to stop it from transmitting malaria. But things get much more complicated when it comes to transmitting this mutation to the millions of mosquitoes buzzing around out there. Unfortunately, we can't just edit a few

mosquitoes and expect them to take over the natural population, for two main reasons:

1 **The *FREP1* mutation is autosomal recessive, meaning that both copies of the gene have to be knocked out to stop a mosquito from transmitting malaria. As Mendel discovered with his tall and small pea plants, you can't have a child with a recessive trait unless you mate with someone who's also a carrier of the same recessive trait (see "How's It Inherited?," page 28). This means that when our gene-edited mosquito mates in nature, it's unlikely to have offspring that are also malaria-resistant.**

2 **To make matters worse, mosquitoes with no *FREP1* protein tend to be weaker than mosquitoes with *FREP1*. They don't drink as much blood or lay as many eggs— which means they're not going to produce as many mosquito babies as their friends with *FREP1*. Fewer babies means less chance of passing on their resistance to malaria.**

So, if you can't get wild mosquitoes to inherit malaria-resistance from knockout mosquitoes, what's the next step? You can't exactly gather up all the mosquitoes in the wild, take them to the lab, and treat them with CRISPR. And breeding mosquitoes in the lab isn't the answer either; scientists estimate that we'd have to release ten lab mosquitoes for every one wild mosquito in order for them to take over.

▌ The Gene Drive Solution

Turns out that science has a solution to this problem—something called a gene drive: technology that can control inheritance by increasing the chance that a certain version of a gene will be passed on, allowing it to spread more quickly through a population. Here's how it works: Cas9 goes into the mosquito with guide RNA of the *FREP1* gene and does its thing, knocking out *FREP1*. But in a gene-drive application, Cas9 would also carry a "gene drive" DNA segment, which includes a template to trigger the find-and-replace mechanism. In this case, the sequence we want inserted at the site of *FREP1* are the genes that code for the Cas9 complex itself.

Sounds crazy, right? But remember—Cas9 is really just a programmable protein. And proteins are made from genes. So, after *FREP1* is knocked out, Cas9 inserts the instructions necessary for the cell to make copies of Cas9. In other words, Cas9 clones itself—complete with guide RNA and the template necessary to make more and more Cas9—passing on the gene drive.

❶ Find and cut: If a mosquito with a gene drive mates with a wild mosquito, the offspring will inherit one chromosome with the gene drive and one wild chromosome without the gene drive. The gene-drive chromosome makes Cas9, which will find and cut DNA on the chromosome without the gene drive based on the gRNA.

❷ Repair and replace: The cell will repair the cut DNA using the gene drive as a template. Now both chromosomes will contain the gene drive, meaning that each one has the genes to make more Cas9.

❸ Spread: Because the gene drive inserts itself into any wild DNA it pairs with, a single copy from one parent is enough to spread the gene drive—and all of the cas genes that come with it—to any children.

The Gene Drive at Work

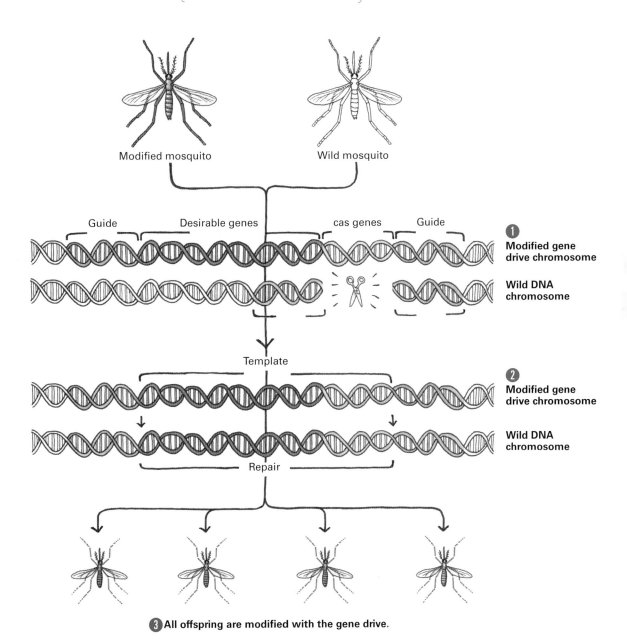

Modified mosquito   Wild mosquito

Guide   Desirable genes   cas genes   Guide

1 Modified gene drive chromosome

Wild DNA chromosome

Template

2 Modified gene drive chromosome

Wild DNA chromosome

Repair

3 All offspring are modified with the gene drive.

Now, the instructions for creating Cas9 are part of the mosquito's genome. Every time the mosquito passes on the chromosome coding for Cas9 instead of *FREP1*, its offspring will produce a Cas9 complex that will genetically edit the chromosome it inherited from the other parent. Instead of following the regular rules of inheritance—in this case, autosomal recessive—all the offspring of the gene-drive mosquito will be resistant to malaria.

Scientists estimate that if we put a malaria-resistance gene drive in just 1 percent of *Anopheles* mosquitoes (one of the types that carries the malaria parasite), it would spread to the entire population within 12 generations. Since mosquitoes are fast breeders, that means new cases of malaria could be eliminated within one year.

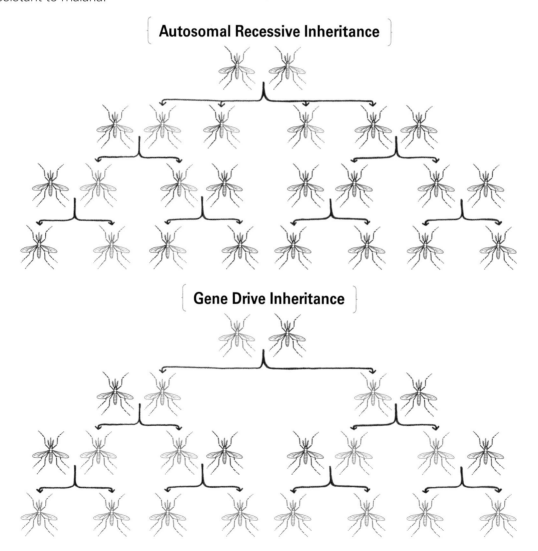

Autosomal Recessive Inheritance

Gene Drive Inheritance

Instead of going through all the trouble of making mosquitoes resistant to disease, why don't we just get rid of them altogether?

Or at least the types that carry malaria? Or at least the females of those species?

A CRISPR gene drive could actually accomplish both these things by knocking out the *doublesex* gene, which makes a protein necessary for female mosquitoes to develop female parts (yes, female mosquitoes do have female parts!). If every *doublesex* gene gets knocked out by Cas9 clones, future generations of mosquitoes will all be male. This would get rid of malaria (remember, the boys don't bite) and eventually wipe out the entire species (because mating requires, well . . . a mate).

This is the type of thinking that keeps those opposed to gene drives awake at night. Sure, mosquitoes are annoying and don't seem to do anything important (besides keeping bug spray companies in business), but should humans really get to decide whether an entire species will live or die? Who decides which pests are pesty enough to get rid of, and who makes sure the technology is limited to bugs?

And while we're deciding who gets to make these decisions, let's not forget that mosquitoes don't carry passports. They're not required to stop at the border and ask for permission to enter a country. What if Tanzania thinks an *FREP1* gene drive is a good way to eliminate malaria, but Kenya thinks the risks are too great?

Because there are risks. Risks serious enough that some people have called for a ban on releasing malaria-resistance gene-drive mosquitoes into the wild until the global community—researchers, politicians, the general public, and future generations—can agree on limitations and regulations. In the meantime, it could be argued that money and resources are better spent on proven methods of malaria reduction such as vaccines, medicines, and mosquito nets.

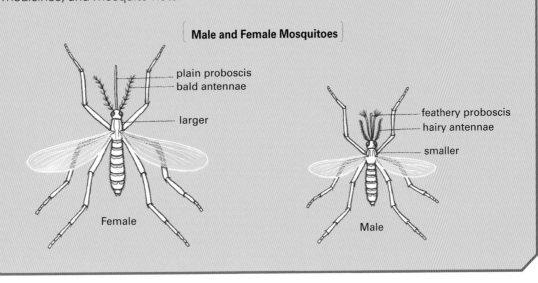

Male and Female Mosquitoes

plain proboscis
bald antennae

larger

Female

feathery proboscis
hairy antennae

smaller

Male

Currently available methods of malaria prevention are far from perfect.

The malaria vaccine is not completely effective and only works temporarily; anti-malarial medications are expensive and have side effects; and mosquito nets are not always used properly and are usually coated with insecticide. Despite efforts to increase the availability of all three, the mosquito causes more human suffering than any other creature on earth. And CRISPR could be the solution.

In addition to malaria, CRISPR-Cas9 gene drives could be used to eliminate other mosquito-borne viruses such as yellow fever, dengue, West Nile, Zika, and chikungunya (see "The World's Deadliest Creature," page 47) without the use of toxic pesticides. What we learn from gene-drive mosquitoes could also be used to genetically edit ticks so they can no longer carry the bacteria that causes Lyme disease. Or bats, so they no longer carry rabies.

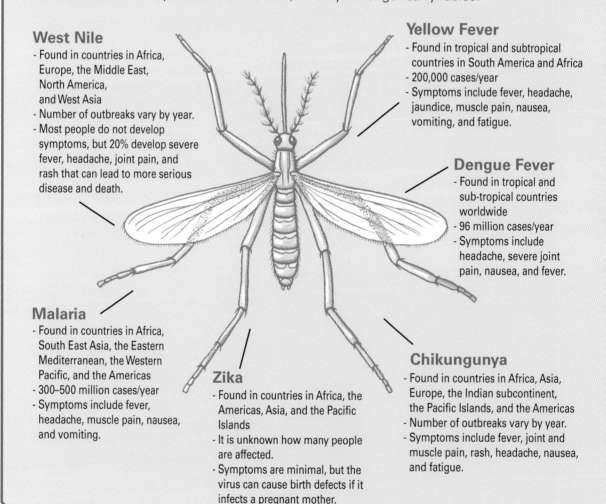

West Nile
- Found in countries in Africa, Europe, the Middle East, North America, and West Asia
- Number of outbreaks vary by year.
- Most people do not develop symptoms, but 20% develop severe fever, headache, joint pain, and rash that can lead to more serious disease and death.

Yellow Fever
- Found in tropical and subtropical countries in South America and Africa
- 200,000 cases/year
- Symptoms include fever, headache, jaundice, muscle pain, nausea, vomiting, and fatigue.

Dengue Fever
- Found in tropical and sub-tropical countries worldwide
- 96 million cases/year
- Symptoms include headache, severe joint pain, nausea, and fever.

Malaria
- Found in countries in Africa, South East Asia, the Eastern Mediterranean, the Western Pacific, and the Americas
- 300–500 million cases/year
- Symptoms include fever, headache, muscle pain, nausea, and vomiting.

Zika
- Found in countries in Africa, the Americas, Asia, and the Pacific Islands
- It is unknown how many people are affected.
- Symptoms are minimal, but the virus can cause birth defects if it infects a pregnant mother.

Chikungunya
- Found in countries in Africa, Asia, Europe, the Indian subcontinent, the Pacific Islands, and the Americas
- Number of outbreaks vary by year.
- Symptoms include fever, joint and muscle pain, rash, headache, nausea, and fatigue.

Sounds good, right? But with this type of power also comes great concern about how it will be used. Those in favor of developing gene-drive technology are quick to point out that it does have natural limitations: It only works in organisms that reproduce with speed and through mating. Gene drives can't be used to engineer, say, a superbug (more about these in chapter 5) because viruses and bacteria reproduce asexually—no mate is required, so an offspring is basically a clone of the parent. Gene drives are also useless in species with long reproductive cycles, such as humans or elephants. If you put a gene drive in an elephant—whose pregnancies typically last more than two years and produce only one baby—it would take centuries for a new trait to spread widely enough to matter.

Gene drives represent a powerful new technology that could allow humans to not only understand evolution but also control it. Using it to combat malaria might be frightening, but it could also prevent human suffering and save millions of lives. And that's reason enough for some people to give CRISPR gene drives the green light.

725,000

475,000

The World's Deadliest Creature

What's the first animal that comes to mind when you think fierce, dangerous, and *deadly*? The shark? The lion? Perhaps you're willing to look in the mirror and guess "human being"?

Nope. If we're talking about the creature that kills more humans than any other, the answer is . . . drum roll, please . . . the mosquito. No other animal even comes close.

What's so deadly about the measly mosquito? It's not the sting itself but what comes with the bite. In addition to malaria, mosquitoes transmit a number of other diseases by dining on someone who's affected and then having an after-dinner snack from an unaffected person.

50,000

25,000

10,000

10,000

10,000

2,500

| Mosquito | Human | Snake | Dog | Tsetse fly | Assassin bug | Freshwater snail | Ascaris roundworm |

CRISPR gene drives have the potential to save many lives but we must proceed with caution.

Gene-drive technology puts society into totally new territory. Instead of genetically editing a single organism, we're talking about changing an entire species. Many experiments have been done using CRISPR-Cas9 to create malaria-resistant mosquitoes in the lab, but there are still lots of questions about what might happen if gene-drive mosquitoes are released into the wild.

What if we wipe out mosquitoes only to find out that they were more important than we realized? If you get rid of all the mosquitoes in a rain forest, the birds that eat them could probably fill their bellies with other insects. And the plants that rely on mosquitoes as pollinators would likely be pollinated by other birds and insects. But in the Arctic, it might be a different story. Wiping out the Arctic mosquito (either on purpose or accidentally through the flow of genes from an anti-malarial gene-drive species to an Arctic species) could have serious consequences—from decreasing the number of birds nesting in the tundra to changing the migratory paths of caribou.

And what if gene-edited mosquitoes emerge stronger than ever? Or change in a way we don't anticipate? We're talking about altering natural selection and evolution (see "Darwin and the Theory of Natural Selection," page 49) in a species that's been on the earth for more than 100 million years. Mammoth people-eating mosquitoes may sound like the plot of a low-budget horror movie, but the point is this: once we release gene-drive mosquitoes into the wild, we lose control over all the potential "what-ifs."

For this reason, scientists are trying to develop safeguards for this technology, such as:

- **precision drives that target DNA sequences unique to a specific species**
- **immunizing drives that make wild mosquitoes resistant to the original gene drive**
- **self-regulating gene drives that die out after a few generations**
- **reversal gene drives that can restore the original sequence**
- **follow-on gene drives that can overwrite unwanted changes**

Each one of these safeguards could act as a type of kill switch, allowing us to stop (or even reverse) the gene drive if something goes wrong. Before we release gene drives into the wild, we must make sure these kill switches are ready to go. And let's also be sure that gene drives are safe enough that we're unlikely to need them.

Darwin and the Theory of Natural Selection

In 1859, Charles Darwin published a book called *On the Origin of Species*, which introduced the world to the theory of evolution by natural selection. This theory describes how plants and animals change over time as a result of changes in heritable traits.

For over 200,000 years, humans have adapted to their environments. What will we look like 200,000 years from now? Will we still be able to hunt or farm? Or will we be permanently attached to our devices?

The basic idea? An organism that changes in a way that allows it to better adapt to its environment is more likely to survive and produce offspring. The tree frog, for example, can be either green or gray. If it lives in the rain forest, being green helps it blend in with a tree's bright green leaves, making it difficult for hungry snakes and birds to see it. But in northern forests, being green makes the tree frog stand out like a target for hungry predators. In this environment, gray coloring provides a selective advantage by allowing the tree frog to blend in with the dry bark of the trees.

Where do these types of changes—or adaptations—come from? Our trusty genes. Remember in chapter 3 when we talked about how mistakes can be made every time our DNA is copied? Sometimes these mistakes are happy accidents. Like the code of a gene that used to produce green pigment being mutated so that it makes gray pigment instead.

As the tree frogs demonstrate, whether a change is good or bad could depend on where you live. In chapter 3, we learned that having sickle cell trait gives you an advantage in places where there's a high risk of malaria. But in other parts of the world? It only increases the chance of having a child with sickle cell anemia.

CUTTING QUESTIONS

PEST CONTROL?

At some point in human history, people stopped relying solely on adaptation to adjust to their environments. Instead, we started changing the environment to suit our needs.

In some cases, changing the environment includes changing the species that share our space. Rather than letting nature decide which plants live where, for example, we choose specific varieties to grow in our gardens—where we control factors such as water and fertilizer and eliminate things like "pests" and competition from "weeds." With a CRISPR gene drive, we could accomplish the same thing faster and easier by inserting "fertilizer" genes into the desirable plants and "poison" genes into the pests. We could even genetically edit the pesky mosquito right into extinction.

Some people think that getting rid of an entire species to ensure the survival of our own is going too far; it's even been described as "playing God." Others think that for human evolution to continue, we must use our knowledge and develop technology to control the world around us.

What do you think? Should we control our environments in any way we can or should we let other species take care of themselves?

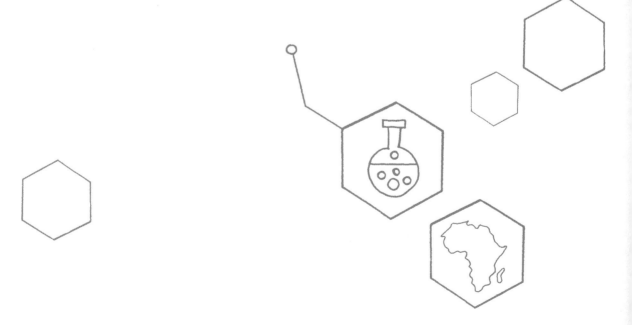

Cancer
CURED

Unlike sickle cell anemia, cancer isn't a single-gene disorder. Although it is a genetic condition, it's never caused by just one single gene mutation. And except in rare cases (see "BRCA," page 63), the mutations are acquired over a person's lifetime; they're not inherited.

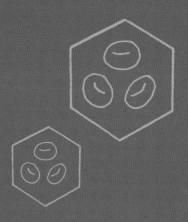

Before becoming deadly, a cancer cell starts out as a regular cell—it could be a skin cell or a lung cell or a stomach cell or . . . you get the idea. As we've talked about, every time the cell makes a copy of the instruction manual in its nucleus, mistakes are made. With a few mistakes, it may still be possible for the cell to follow the instructions provided by the genome. But as mistakes pile up, it can start to look like a science binder that's exploded all over the school hallway.

As the number of mutations build, the cell starts dividing faster and faster—copying all 3 billion of its base pairs every time and accumulating more and more spelling mistakes. This makes it hard for researchers to figure out what mutation caused the cancerous cell to start growing out of control in the first place, which is important information for preventing, diagnosing, and treating specific types of cancers.

It doesn't help that even though the human genome's been sequenced since 2003, we still don't know what a lot of genes do. And we're still in the dark about most of that non-coding DNA we talked about in chapter 2. This is where CRISPR comes in: the technology has helped researchers better understand cancer and other complex diseases.

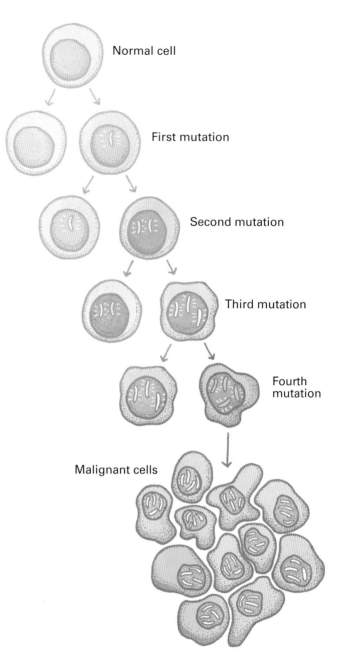

Normal cell

First mutation

Second mutation

Third mutation

Fourth mutation

Malignant cells

DNA mutations can be caused by environmental factors like the sun, radiation, and smoke, or by mistakes made during replication. As more mutations accumulate, cells start growing out of control and eventually become a tumor. A tumor becomes malignant when it starts invading other cells to become a cancer.

▌Knocking Out Cancer?

It's a simple two-step process: knock out a gene and see what happens. Because CRISPR-Cas9 is so accurate and precise, it can also be programmed to knock out multiple genes in different orders to mimic the development of cancer and other complex disorders. At last count, CRISPR had been used to make over 13,000 edits in a single cell!

Not all cancer-causing mutations happen within the gene, however. Just before the three-letter code that tells the cell where a gene starts coding for a protein, there's information in the DNA about when a gene should be turned on or off. Think of it like a light switch that "activates" the gene when protein needs to be made and "inactivates" it when protein isn't necessary. The process of turning a gene on and off is called gene expression.

Since cancer can be caused by mutations that make genes turn on or off at the wrong time, scientists have hacked the CRISPR system to control gene expression as well. In this case, the nuclease within the Cas9 complex is replaced by a type of molecular switch. This version of Cas9 still uses guide RNA to find a matching 20-base-pair sequence, specifically one just before the START of the target gene (a region called the promoter). But instead of snipping the double helix after unwinding it with the helicase, it binds a new protein directly to the DNA. Depending on the protein, this will either activate or repress the gene next to it.

A lot of this research is done in mice because they make excellent models for human disease. Why? They share 85 percent of their genes with humans; have similar immune, nervous, cardiovascular, and musculoskeletal systems; and breed quickly in captivity.

Mouse models of many different cancer types have been created using CRISPR. In addition to helping us understand what causes cancer, mouse models are also being used to help us fight it.

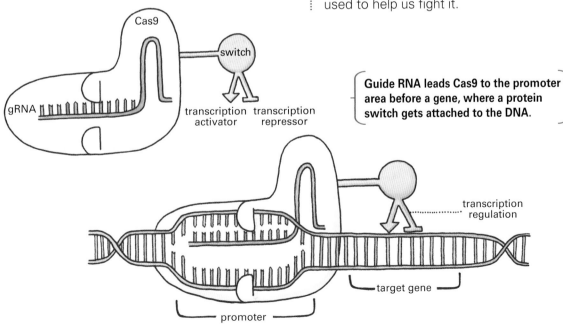

Guide RNA leads Cas9 to the promoter area before a gene, where a protein switch gets attached to the DNA.

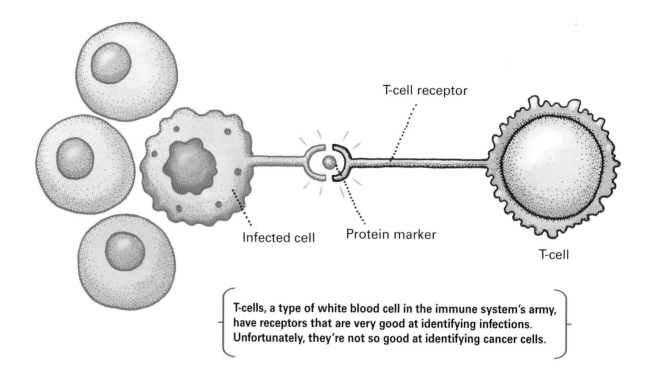

T-cell receptor

Infected cell

Protein marker

T-cell

T-cells, a type of white blood cell in the immune system's army, have receptors that are very good at identifying infections. Unfortunately, they're not so good at identifying cancer cells.

█ Immunotherapy

Here's where things get really interesting. We've used CRISPR to intentionally create a mouse that will develop cancer. Can we now use CRISPR to cure that same mouse?

Logically, it makes sense to cure the cancer the same way it was created. In other words: edit the genes that were mutated in the first place. This might be possible if we treat the mouse in the pre-cancerous stage. But once a tumor starts growing, it's pretty much impossible to fix all the mutations that accumulate with each cell division.

Another option is to edit the cancer cells to make conventional drugs more effective. For example, you can make lung cancer cells more susceptible to chemotherapy

treatment by knocking out just one gene with CRISPR-Cas9. CRISPR can also identify which genes are essential for the survival of a particular cancer so that targeted drugs can be developed.

Still, cancer is a war between cells growing out of control and healthy cells that are fighting off their invasion. So, instead of targeting the cancer cells, what if we help the healthy cells win the war? This is the idea behind immunotherapy—a treatment through which the body's own immune system is equipped to hunt down and kill cancerous cells.

To understand how immunotherapy works, it helps to know a little bit about how cells communicate and interact. Just like we have unique fingerprints, animal cells have proteins in their membranes to help other cells identify them. They also have receptors in their membranes that take signals from what's happening around them—sort of like a submarine periscope that lets a sailor see what's happening above the water—and tell the cell how to react. This identification-and-reaction system allows the cell to do everything from opening the gates (or channels) in the membrane so nutritious molecules can enter to arming itself for a fight against an enemy like bacteria or virus. Cancer cells are experts at hiding from T-cells—the immune system's primary foot soldiers. They use a variety of tricks to do this, from hiding their protein identity markers to releasing molecules that put T-cells to sleep. (Cancer cells don't exactly fight fair!)

T-cells have been engineered in a number of ways to help them beat the stealthy cancer cells. One way relies on assistance from another member of the immune team: B-cells. The B-cell's superpower is identifying a certain type of protein in the cancer cell membrane. But B-cells don't have the killing power of T-cells. Put them together? You've got yourself a super T-cell killing machine.

To make this system even more effective, the engineered super T-cell can be made to order for a patient's specific cancer profile (kind of like a dating profile that highlights the bad stuff—gene mutations—instead of the good). In mouse models, CRISPR has made T-cell engineering faster, cheaper, and more accurate. Accuracy is a particularly important feature, because once a T-cell is armed, it will hunt the enemy relentlessly. CRISPR has also allowed researchers to try this form of immunotherapy on different types of cancer, including blood, brain, and lung cancer.

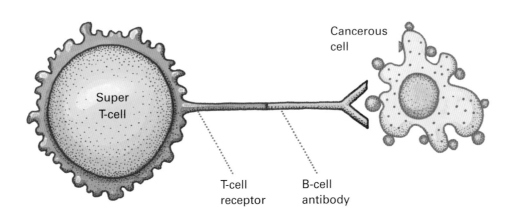

Cancerous cell

Super T-cell

T-cell receptor

B-cell antibody

Engineered T-cell receptors with extra B-cell recognition power will signal the super T-cell to fight against the cancer cell.

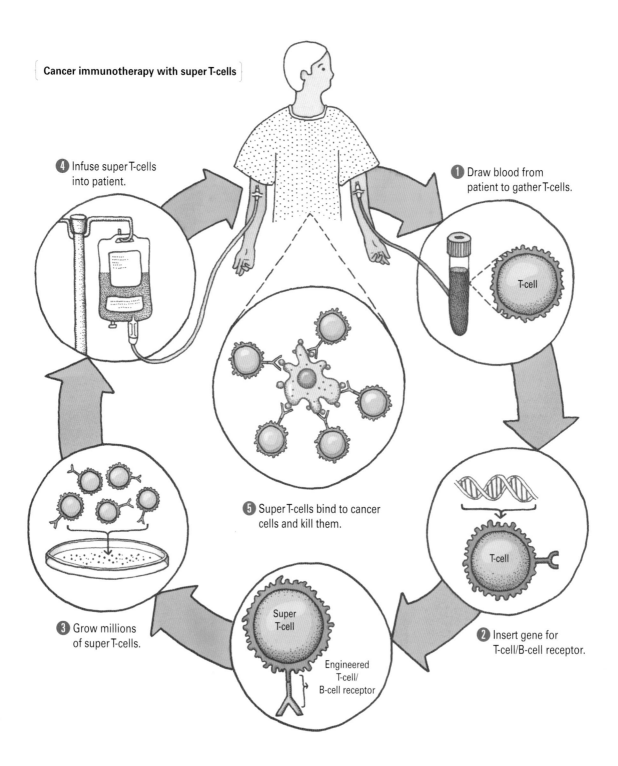

Cancer immunotherapy with super T-cells

4 Infuse super T-cells into patient.

1 Draw blood from patient to gather T-cells.

T-cell

5 Super T-cells bind to cancer cells and kill them.

T-cell

3 Grow millions of super T-cells.

Super T-cell

Engineered T-cell/ B-cell receptor

2 Insert gene for T-cell/B-cell receptor.

A Bioweapon War?

A bioweapon is a living organism designed to attack another living thing. It could be a toxin that's poisonous to specific plants or animals. It could also be an infectious agent like a virus or bacteria. There are a few different ways that CRISPR could be used to edit an organism into a biological weapon.

Bioterror trick #1: Superbugs. Through natural selection (see "Darwin and the Theory of Natural Selection," page 49), some bacteria survive because of random mutations that make them resistant to the drugs designed to kill them. Using CRISPR, the bacterial genome could be intentionally edited to resist antibiotics, leading to infectious diseases that cannot be treated.

CRISPR could also be used to recreate a virus like smallpox, which was responsible for 300–500 million deaths before it was officially eradicated throughout the world in 1980. Although there is a vaccine for smallpox, if the virus (or an imitation of the virus) were to be released today, it would spread very quickly because very few people have natural immunity.

Bioterror trick #2: Biochemicals. Using CRISPR, a cell's genome could be edited to produce proteins that are capable of destroying the very cell that made them. The genome could also be edited so that the cell can no longer produce the workers required to perform tasks necessary for its survival. In either case, the edited cells would eventually die off until there was nothing left.

Going one step further, if a T-cell can be programmed to find and destroy cancer cells based on unique proteins in the cell membrane, it can also be programmed to find and destroy cells based on proteins specific to a person's ancestry, gender, or family. Using this technology, a biological toxin could be engineered that's poisonous to specific groups of people.

Not many people would argue against using every weapon we have to fight the war on cancer.

One in every two to three people will develop cancer during their lifetime. In North America, the only cause of death more common than cancer is heart disease.

But there are other reasons to pursue this type of research as well.

First, animal models can do a lot more than just create mice with cancer. To study other complex human conditions, scientists are working on everything from monkeys with depression to rabbits prone to obesity. CRISPR can even edit animals to produce pharmaceuticals or make pigs into human organ donors.

Second, using CRISPR-Cas9 to treat cancer with immunotherapy has given us a powerful new tool in the fight against HIV (see "A Sneak Attack," page 59). Gene editing of cell receptors could also stop viruses like the one that causes Covid-19 from entering human cells and causing infection.

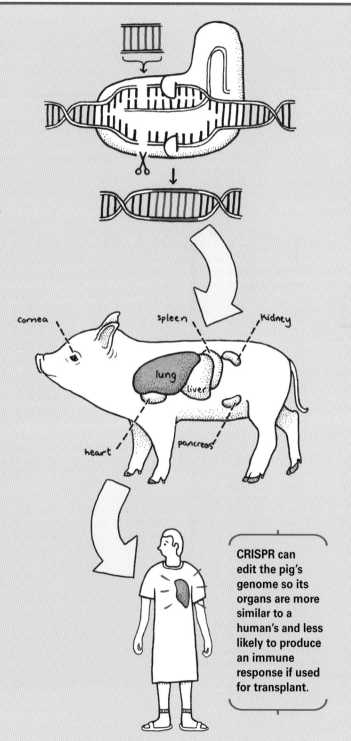

cornea   spleen   kidney

lung   liver

heart   pancreas

CRISPR can edit the pig's genome so its organs are more similar to a human's and less likely to produce an immune response if used for transplant.

Finally, what we learn about controlling gene expression with CRISPR could eventually be used to create antibiotics that fight specific bacteria, which could solve the problem of antibiotic resistance (see "A Bioweapon War?," page 57). It may even be possible to create a type of B-cell vaccine that would get rid of the need for antibiotics altogether.

A Sneak Attack

The human immunodeficiency virus—more commonly known as HIV—causes acquired immunodeficiency syndrome, or AIDS. How? By attacking a specific type of T-cell called CD4.

In a sneaky maneuver, HIV invades CD4 T-cells by disguising itself with proteins the T-cell doesn't recognize as a threat. Once HIV enters a T-cell through its receptor—or doorway—the virus incorporates its DNA into the T-cell's genome where it grows and divides and eventually wipes out the entire T-cell army, making the body unable to fight off infections from other bugs.

To stop this HIV invasion, CRISPR-Cas9 can edit the T-cell's genome so it no longer has the receptor HIV uses to get in. No more door? No more AIDS.

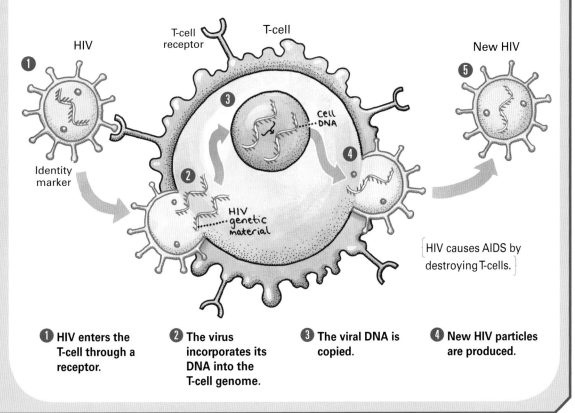

HIV causes AIDS by destroying T-cells.

❶ **HIV enters the T-cell through a receptor.**   ❷ **The virus incorporates its DNA into the T-cell genome.**   ❸ **The viral DNA is copied.**   ❹ **New HIV particles are produced.**

Before CRISPR can be used to treat cancer in humans, we need to make sure it's both safe and effective.

This means some big things need to be figured out before any of these treatments are made available to humans.

As mentioned in chapter 3, there's a concern that CRISPR-Cas9 could actually cause cancer through off-target knockouts or errors made by the cell's repair system. Not surprisingly, both of these risks increase when multiple genes are edited at once. In addition to addressing these issues, scientists are working on better ways to deliver the Cas9 complex to cells.

Right now, the most common way for Cas9 to get into a cell is to hitch a ride with that ancient bacterial enemy—the virus. Viruses are good carriers because they make a living off of infecting cells and incorporating their own DNA into their hosts' genomes. The viruses used in gene editing don't cause disease in humans because the viral genes have been removed to create something called a vector. But viral vectors still have limitations: they can only carry a small amount of DNA, they stick around for a long time, they can produce an immune response, and they sometimes start messing with the DNA in places they have no right to be.

For all of these reasons, scientists are working on alternative ways for Cas9 to catch a ride into target cells. Some alternative delivery mechanisms include:

- **Nanoparticles:** The idea behind this method is to wrap Cas9 into a super-tiny package that gets piggybacked into the cell on the back of something that can easily travel through the channels in the cell membrane, like a fat molecule or gold particle.

- **Light:** This method also uses nanoparticles, but in this case, they're light-activated. Once inside the nucleus, the nanoparticles hang on to Cas9 until light is shone on the cell. Only then is Cas9 set free to get to work editing genes.

- **Electric shock:** A zap of electricity can relax cells enough to let Cas9 in without the need for any vehicle at all.

- **Microinjection:** Exactly as it sounds, this method involves giving the cell an injection with a microscopic needle. Microinjection is commonly used to create animal models. In plants, the CRISPR system is more likely to be blasted directly into the cell with a gene gun.

Choosing the best delivery vehicle depends on what cell type you're targeting and whether it's inside the body or out. When using CRISPR to treat human disease, it's important to make sure the Cas9 package is delivered to the right place; miss, and the therapy could have unintended consequences (we don't want to knock out receptors in the wrong immune cells, for example). Ideally, doctors would also like to have a "kill switch" (see chapter 4) to control Cas9 once it gets into the cell. That way, it could be shut down if anything goes wrong or when it's no longer needed.

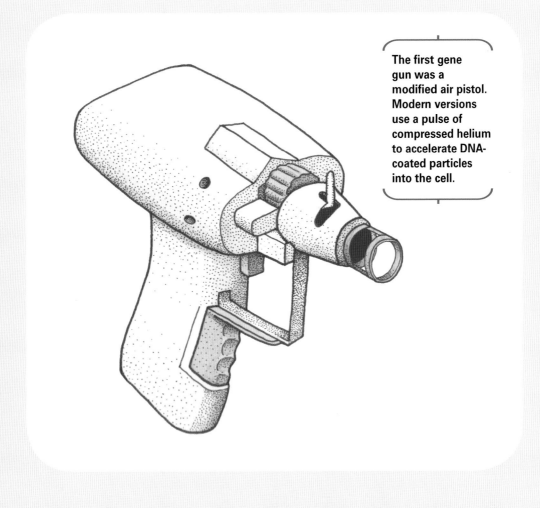

The first gene gun was a modified air pistol. Modern versions use a pulse of compressed helium to accelerate DNA-coated particles into the cell.

STOP

Researchers are confident CRISPR-Cas9 will not be used to treat cancer in humans until there's proof that it won't cause more cancer than it cures.

And while this confidence is not necessarily naive—government organizations will not give their seals of approval without rigorous scientific study—there's still cause for concern.

Biotech companies—which use living organisms to produce drugs and other products—are some of the biggest traded companies on the stock market today. In fact, some are so invested in CRISPR that they've worked the technology into their names! And each of the three largest publicly traded CRISPR companies has over $1 billion invested in them, even though they are all just in the research and development phase. (In other words, they don't have anything to sell. Yet.)

If these companies are not successful in bringing their genetically edited products to market, might they start exploring more profitable uses for their technology? Start selling to the highest bidder, regardless of the buyer's intent? Here's where we could fall off the slippery slope and get caught up in an avalanche instead.

U.S. intelligence officials have referred to gene editing as a potential weapon of mass destruction. The main concern? Bioweapons (see "A Bioweapon War?," page 57).

From genetically engineered super-viruses to biological weapons that target people with specific DNA sequences, the threat is real. CRISPR, like many technologies, has the potential to be used for both good and evil. But the idea that CRISPR is easy and cheap enough to be used by a common terrorist is an extreme exaggeration. If you have no scientific background, there are easier ways to cause a lot of damage. But for the researcher who's spent his life—and his fortune—on genetic editing, it may be a different story.

Beyond this fear of how a mad scientist facing bankruptcy could start (or end) the next world war, there's the very real fact that CRISPR technology is progressing at a pace that's never been seen before in the biomedical field. It's hard for the regulators to keep up with the rapid pace of development. Especially since they're under a lot of pressure from shareholders that are banking on the success of a company's product.

How do we make sure that regulators do their jobs properly? And if a CRISPR treatment does get approved, how do we educate everyone on the potential harms and benefits?

All medicine has side effects. (We've all seen those crazy TV commercials listing all of the things that *might* happen if you take a certain medication. Yikes!) But with that type of medication, the side effects usually disappear once you stop taking it. With CRISPR-Cas9, errors are incorporated *into the human genome.* This means that not only is the change permanent, but it also gets copied every time that cell divides. Scary stuff.

BRCA

BRCA1 and BRCA2 are human genes that produce tumor suppressor proteins. They work to repair DNA damage—specifically, breaks in the double helix caused by radiation or other environmental exposures. If not repaired, this type of damage eventually turns the genome into that disorganized and totally unreadable science binder we talked about at the beginning of the chapter.

BRCA1 and BRCA2 are not the only tumor suppressor genes. (The cells need a lot of repair proteins to keep up with all the different types of damage that occur over a person's lifetime!) But they are two of only a few different genes associated with an increase in cancer risk that's inherited.

Someone who inherits a mutation in one copy of either their BRCA1 or BRCA2 gene is missing the tumor suppressor proteins their cells are supposed to make. They will not necessarily develop cancer—other mutations still need to accumulate over their lifetime to cause a cell to become cancerous. But they do have an increased risk of both breast and ovarian cancer.

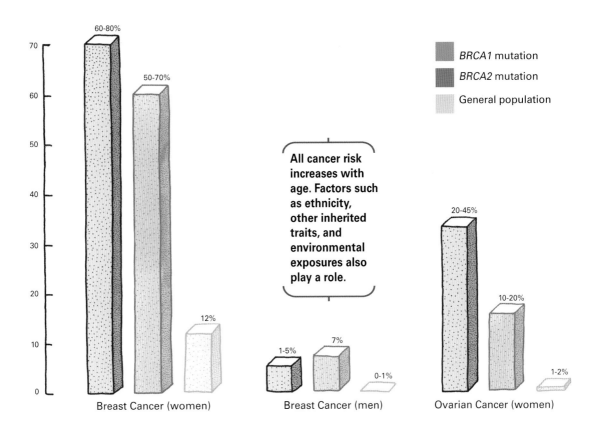

Less than 5 percent of all cancer is associated with an inherited mutation in a single gene like BRCA1 or BRCA2. But if there's a lot of a cancer in a family—present in every generation, starting in the same primary cell type (breast or bowel, for example), and occurring at a young age—genetic counseling and testing can be done to help determine a person's risk.

CUTTING QUESTIONS

ANIMAL TESTING

Over the last 100 years, animal testing has led to almost every medical breakthrough—from vaccines to drugs to surgical interventions. Some people believe it's both cruel and immoral to make animals suffer for the benefit of humans. Others say that animal testing is necessary and acceptable if it prevents human suffering when no other options are available.

What do you think? Should we use animals to develop technologies like CRISPR to improve human health?

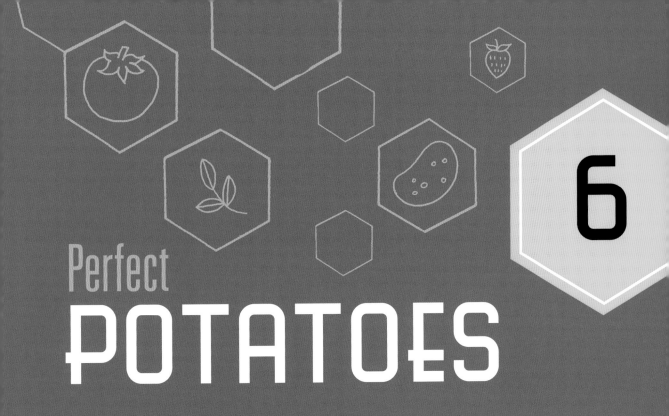

Perfect
POTATOES

Let's take a break from disease to talk about something a little more appetizing: food! Stay tuned, because CRISPR is coming soon to a plate near you!

Among all the potential ways we might use gene editing, this is the way it's likely to happen first. Why? Because our food supply is already heavily genetically modified.

There are different opinions on what a genetically modified organism—or GMO—is (see "What Exactly Is Genetic Engineering?," page 21), but there's no arguing that GMOs are already part of our food chain. In fact, some estimates suggest that up to 75 percent of processed foods sold in North American grocery stores contain genetically modified ingredients. And over 90 percent of the largest global crops—including corn, soybeans, and cotton—are genetically engineered.

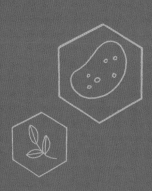

▌A-Plus for Potatoes

Scientists around the world are now applying gene-editing techniques to another top crop that's important to everyone from junk food enthusiasts to fans of French cuisine: the potato. Potatoes are known for being easy to grow—and are grown pretty much everywhere on earth—but growing the tasty tubers on a mass scale can be a risky venture.

In the field, potato crops are under attack by viruses, bacteria, and fungi. Researchers have been tinkering with the potato genome for decades to try to make them resistant to blight, which can be caused by any of these threats—most often by inserting DNA from another species to create what's known as a transgenic organism. With CRISPR, we may be able to accomplish this resistance by knocking a few genes out of the potato's own genome instead.

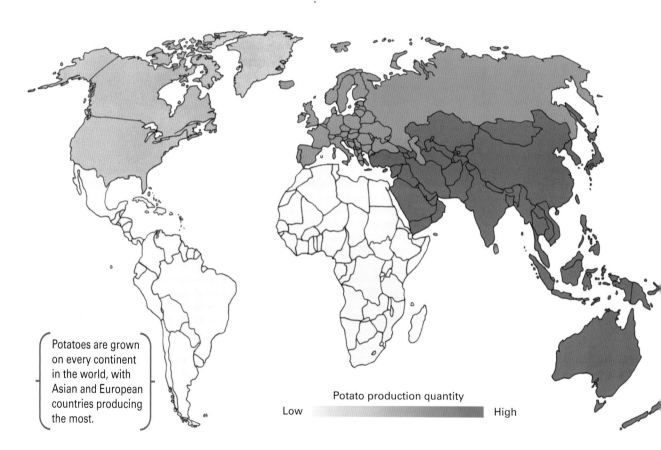

Potatoes are grown on every continent in the world, with Asian and European countries producing the most.

Potato production quantity

Low   High

This is a big plus for both farmers and consumers, since blight-resistant potatoes can be grown without the need for pesticides. In Europe and North America, it would limit—or even eliminate—the need for chemical sprays, which would be great for the health of both people and the environment. And in the many countries that can't afford costly pesticides, a CRISPR potato could literally save lives by preventing future famine.

CRISPR can also help once the potato is picked. Tubers are often stored for long periods of time before they are shipped or eaten. During storage, the starches in the potato naturally convert to sugar—a process referred to as "cold-induced sweetening." In itself, this isn't a problem (especially if you have a sweet tooth!). The problem comes up when the potato gets cooked at high heat—a must if you're trying to make crispy potato chips or french fries. At high temperatures, the sugar gets converted into acrylamide, a chemical that disrupts the normal function of nerve cells and may possibly cause cancer.

With CRISPR-Cas9, the single gene that converts the potato's starch to sugar during that period of cold-induced sweetening can be knocked out. When this was done in Ranger Russet potatoes, researchers reported a 70 percent drop in acrylamide. In addition, the gene-edited spuds did not brown when made into chips—another big plus for both farmers and foodies.

Selective Breeding vs. Crossbreeding

Most of us don't think much about how plants breed (or even the fact that plants breed at all). But like humans, plants need to pass on their genetic material to the next generation. And humans being . . . well, *human* . . . have found a way to influence this process.

Selective breeding involves choosing what plant will parent the next generation (since most plants have both male and female parts, only one parent is required) based on a desirable trait: re-planting the tuber of one potato in a crop of thousands, for example, because it's bigger or sweeter or less buggy than the others. It's not that much different than natural selection, as described by Darwin (see "Darwin and the Theory of Natural Selection," page 49), but it's controlled by humans rather than nature. Traits that are desirable to humans are not necessarily the same as those that help plants or animals survive in the wild.

Crossbreeding is the process of bringing two unrelated parents together to create something new. This is what Mendel was doing when he mated tall pea plants with small pea plants. Another example would be applying the pollen of a big potato plant to the flower of a disease-resistant potato plant to try to produce a super potato with desirable traits from both parents.

▌A Safer Spud?

Even without cold storage, potatoes contain solanine. This natural toxin—which helps protect the potato from insects—can increase with exposure to light and warm temperatures, causing the skin to take on a distinctly greenish tinge. If you happen to come across a potato that bears a striking resemblance to the Grinch or the Incredible Hulk, steer clear: eating it could leave you facing bouts of vomiting and diarrhea.

Not surprisingly, most green potatoes are tossed before they ever make it to the grocery store, and most people know to store potatoes in cool, dark places and throw away the ones that start turning green once you get them home. Wouldn't it be nice, though, if farmers and food producers and consumers didn't have to worry about potentially poisonous potatoes? That's where CRISPR comes in. It can be programmed to knock out the gene—*CYP88B1*—that codes for the protein that makes solanine. Do that, and green potatoes will be a thing of the past—a major advantage for people who eat (or sell) the popular tuber.

CRISPR could also be used to make potatoes more nutritious and possibly even more delicious. For example, potatoes are high in starch—which means they're often avoided by people following a low-carbohydrate diet. Could a CRISPR-Cas9 system be used to decrease the starch in potatoes and increase the amount of nutrients such as vitamin C, vitamin B6, and magnesium? There's a good chance a scientist somewhere is researching it. And while we're imagining possible potato-related applications for CRISPR, perhaps the flavor could be enhanced to suit the taste buds of consumers around the world by increasing the expression of some potato genes and decreasing the expression of others.

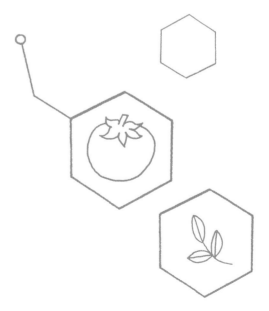

Who Owns CRISPR?

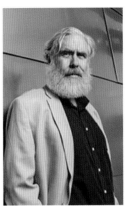

With a technology as valuable as CRISPR, the question of who "owns" it—or, more accurately, who "invented" it—is an expensive one. Tens of millions of dollars have been spent in the courts trying to figure it out, and the battle's not over yet.

It's been a heavyweight fight between two main groups. In one end of the ring is Jennifer Doudna, who works at the University of California (UC), Berkeley, and Emmanuelle Charpentier, currently employed by the Max Planck Institute for Infection Biology in Berlin, Germany. Together, these scientists published the first scientific paper describing how CRISPR could be transformed into a gene-editing tool in the June 2012 edition of *Science*. In 2015, they were awarded the $3 million Breakthrough Prize in Life Sciences, and *Time* magazine listed the duo among the 100 most influential people in the world. One year later, the CRISPR pioneers were runners-up for *Time* magazine's Person of the Year.

At the other end of the ring is Feng Zhang from the Broad Institute of MIT and Harvard. In January 2013, his team published research proving that gene editing worked in mouse and human cells. On the sidelines is his former supervisor, George Church, whose Harvard-based lab independently reported developing CRISPR-based human-cell gene editing in the same issue of *Science* that Zhang's lab did.

Everyone was so excited about CRISPR's potential that they formed independent companies to capitalize on its success. And both teams filed patent applications before their findings were published. Here's where things get interesting (and messy). Zhang paid extra to get his patent application examined quickly, so he was initially granted valuable claims to CRISPR in the United States. Feeling sucker-punched, UC Berkeley fought back on behalf of both Doudna and Charpentier, arguing that Zhang's work on CRISPR was just an extension of their initial discovery.

Both groups will likely be granted some patent rights, but the devil is in the details—in this case, which CRISPR-Cas9 technology gets included in each claim and whether the word *cellular* is included or not.

For most of us, it's a battle that leaves us scratching our heads. But for the CRISPR scientists? They're more likely to be running to the bank, regardless of who wins the race.

Is your mouth watering for an acrylamide-free, solanine-free, starchless potato with natural sour-cream-and-onion flavoring? Or maybe seaweed and sesame-seasoned chips are more to your liking? You never know; it could happen. And there are many other ways fruits and vegetables can be genetically edited. Here are some possibilities to chew on:

- peanuts with the allergen snipped out
- wheat with gluten that can be tolerated by people with celiac disease
- mushrooms that don't brown or bruise when cut
- corn crops that continue to grow even without water
- mini tomatoes to feed astronauts in space
- sweeter strawberries with a longer shelf life
- soybean oil with more healthy fats and less trans fat
- bananas and sweet potatoes with extra beta-carotene (to help the body make vitamin A, which is necessary for the immune system but lacking in some diets, particularly of those who live in some African countries, such as Ghana)

The Flavr Savr Tomato

You've probably never heard of the Flavr Savr tomato, but in the mid-1990s it made headline news across the world. The first GMO to be approved for sale in the United States, the Flavr Savr tomato was transgenic—it had a foreign gene inserted into its genome to stop the natural production of a protein involved in the decaying process. Without this protein, the tomato stayed firm for up to three weeks. This was great for farmers and food producers because it meant the tomatoes could be picked when they were red and ripe and still survive the long trip to the grocery store without losing flavor.

Consumer reaction was mixed, however. Even though the Flavr Savr tomato met all the regulatory guidelines, some people were skeptical about eating fruit with foreign genes. It didn't help that it was double the price of a regular tomato, thanks to high production and distribution costs (research is expensive!). And despite the hype, they didn't even taste that great—partly because the company that made them wasn't allowed to genetically modify the top tomato varieties.

A few years after it hit the stores, the Flavr Savr tomato disappeared from the shelves. Today, CRISPR could be used to create a new version of the Flavr Savr tomato—a much cheaper and possibly tastier version. But most producers seem to have bigger and better things in mind such as tomato plants that flower and ripen quicker.

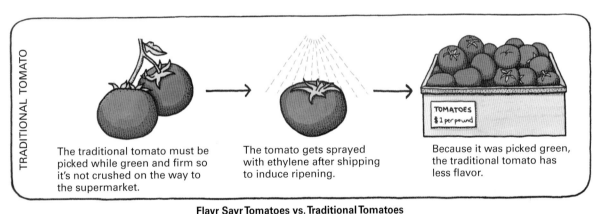

TRADITIONAL TOMATO

The traditional tomato must be picked while green and firm so it's not crushed on the way to the supermarket.

The tomato gets sprayed with ethylene after shipping to induce ripening.

Because it was picked green, the traditional tomato has less flavor.

Flavr Savr Tomatoes vs. Traditional Tomatoes

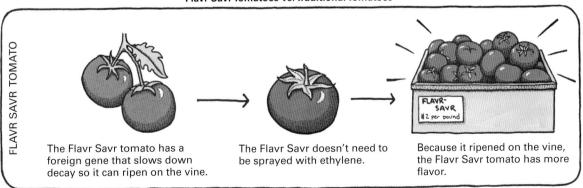

FLAVR SAVR TOMATO

The Flavr Savr tomato has a foreign gene that slows down decay so it can ripen on the vine.

The Flavr Savr doesn't need to be sprayed with ethylene.

Because it ripened on the vine, the Flavr Savr tomato has more flavor.

It's hard to talk about eating a meal made by CRISPR without getting caught up in the debate about GMOs.

We'll address that issue in the Cutting Question at the end of the chapter. For now, it's important to keep in mind that gene editing is much more precise than the technology used to create the first GMOs approved for human consumption in the 1990s.

With CRISPR-Cas9, we're not talking about opening an instruction manual to a random page and stuffing in a bunch of extra letters. We're talking about targeting a specific area of the genome and getting the cell to make changes to its own genetic code.

This means that foreign DNA isn't being inserted into a plant's genome. If the template carried by Cas9 is copied from the code of a different plant or animal, it can be used to make a type of transgenic organism, but even in this case, no foreign DNA is added.

So, instead of introducing a gene from an unrelated species to produce a desired trait—like adding a new chapter to our instruction manual—CRISPR can make subtle changes to what's already there. For example, inactive genes within the tomato genome can be activated using CRISPR to control gene expression. With this technology, we can grow naturally spicy tomatoes—picked ready for easy-to-make salsa—without inserting foreign DNA from the genome of a hot pepper plant.

The European Union—where GMOs must be labeled by law—originally decided that gene-edited plants would be regulated in the same way as their ancestors but has recently started to relax legislation on new breeding methods. In North America, gene-edited crops that don't contain foreign DNA do not require the same strict regulation and testing required for GMOs. And Japan allows gene-edited food to be sold to consumers without any additional safety evaluation at all.

Sound confusing? As with anything GMO related—it is. And for this reason, public education is needed to ensure that consumers can make truly informed decisions about what they're eating.

	CRISPR Gene Editing	Genetically Modified Organisms
DNA origin	DNA native to the plant is altered or removed.	Genes are harvested from another species or are synthetically made.
DNA location	DNA change is made to a specific spot in the genome.	DNA change is inserted at a random location within the genome.
Identification	Modified plants are identical to their traditional counterparts.	Modified plants are distinguishable from traditional plants.
Regulation	Currently, procedures that mimic natural processes are not regulated in the U.S.	GMOs are rigorously regulated by the EPA, FDA, and USDA.

STOP

Regardless of how food is labeled or defined, many people feel that it should not be produced in a lab and worry about consuming anything that's been genetically altered.

They're concerned about the motives of the companies that produce this food, and wonder whether making money is playing a bigger role than making a positive difference.

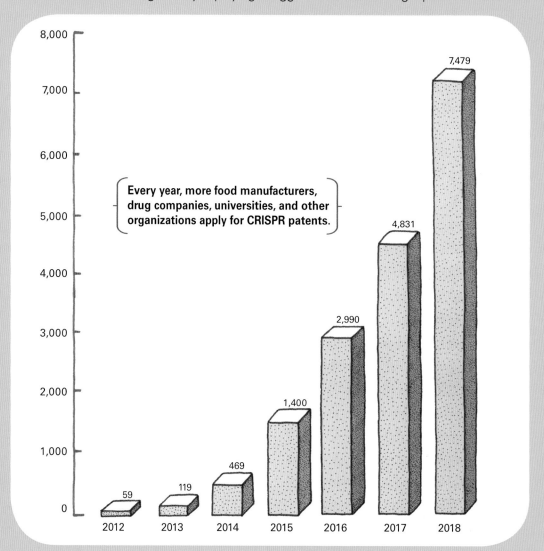

Every year, more food manufacturers, drug companies, universities, and other organizations apply for CRISPR patents.

It's a valid question. As with biotechnology, millions of dollars have been invested in discovering, researching, and developing genetically edited agriculture. And with big money comes big business.

Many for-profit companies have made agreements with universities and other technology developers for the right to use CRISPR-Cas9 in the creation of their products. Huge legal battles have been fought over who owns the rights to these technologies (see "Who Owns CRISPR?," page 69). And the number of CRISPR patent applications rose from 11 in 2008 to 7,479 in 2018—an increase of 680 times in just 10 years—that's a lot of people claiming ownership of different CRISPR technologies!

Big multinational corporations have a lot to gain—and a lot to lose—from society's acceptance of genetically edited food. That means it's up to us to make sure we're being fed the truth. In other words: buyer beware.

When we're told about all the amazing things CRISPR can do to food, we can ask ourselves a few important questions: Is it really an improvement? And who stands to benefit? Farmers? Consumers? Agribusinesses? Sustainable farming systems? Industrial agriculture?

"Pest-free," for example, may be a great supermarket slogan (especially when it refers to something that's going into your salad), but what does it actually mean? Are we talking about a grain that's been genetically modified to be resistant to a specific chemical so herbicides can be used to destroy weeds without killing the crop? Or a fruit that's been genetically edited to be resistant to a specific disease? It could be a change that makes the company that developed it millions of dollars in both seed and herbicide sales. Or it might have the potential to save the entire papaya industry (also worth millions of dollars) from being wiped out by the ring spot virus.

Beyond knowing who will benefit from genetically edited food is the question of whether it will live up to its promises. Does a herbicide-resistant crop really reduce the use of more toxic chemicals? How do we deal with weeds that develop herbicide resistance? What happens when crops resistant to one disease get exposed to another?

In all of these cases, we must also consider how gene-edited crops will affect our entire ecosystem and try to predict their environmental impact over long periods of time. Not an easy job! But it's work that must be done before we can safely—and comfortably—order up that CRISPR salad.

Over 250 scientific and technical organizations around the world support the safety of genetically altered crops.

This includes the National Academy of Sciences, the European Food Safety Authority, the European Commission, Health Canada, the American Medical Association, the Food and Drug Administration, the Food and Agriculture Organization of the United Nations, the World Academy of Sciences, and the World Health Organization. In their opinions—based on scientific studies that have been conducted since GMOs were first introduced to the market—genetically altered crops pose no more risk to humans than those that have been developed by conventional breeding techniques.

Which brings us to another argument in favor of giving a green light to the use of CRISPR-Cas9 in plant cultivation: we're not producing anything different than what selective breeding and crossbreeding have been producing for centuries (see "Selective Breeding vs. Crossbreeding," page 67). We're just doing it in less time. And time could be a huge factor when we consider editing crops to adapt to things like climate change and a rapidly expanding global population.

Right now, there are over 7.5 billion people on the planet, who collectively consume 5 million kilograms (11 million pounds) of food every minute of every single day. With the global population expected to reach almost 10 billion by 2050, we'll need 70 percent more food than we grow today. In the years to come, there will also be more extreme weather events that will severely affect our ability to produce that food.

Advances in agriculture have always been associated with our advancement as a species. During the Green Revolution of the 1950s and '60s (also known as the Third Agricultural Revolution), new high-yielding seed varieties, increased use of fertilizers, and improved irrigation methods had a huge impact on global food production.

At this point in time, gene-editing staple crops to make them drought resistant or cold tolerant or even more nutritious (the Fourth Agricultural Revolution?) may be necessary for our long-term survival. Not only will it help to feed the planet, but it also stands to benefit people living in developing nations—as much (or more) than the Green Revolution—as long as we make sure everyone has access to CRISPR technology.

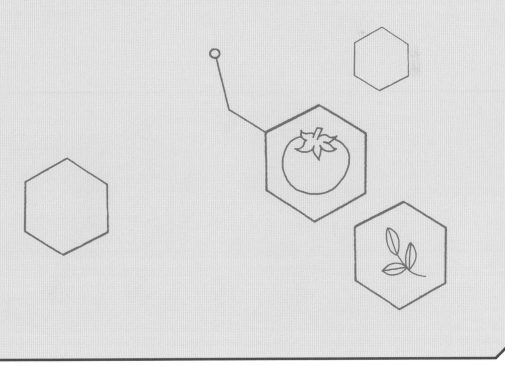

CUTTING QUESTIONS

TO GMO OR NOT TO GMO?

The introduction of GMOs to the supermarket sparked a polarizing debate that continues to rage today. Those against GMOs worry that they could pose a threat to human health. They've lobbied to have GMOs labeled, and some have gone as far as calling them "Frankenfoods." Many people opposed to GMOs believe we should be returning to more natural—or organic—methods of food production rather than supporting huge agribusinesses.

Those in favor of GMOs argue that they've passed more safety testing than any other food. They believe GMOs have become the victim of a vocal minority that spreads misinformation and preys on public distrust of big companies. Some proponents also claim that only privileged members of society can afford to rely on organic food production and that the global community can't support a growing population without genetic technology.

What do you think? What's your opinion on GMOs?

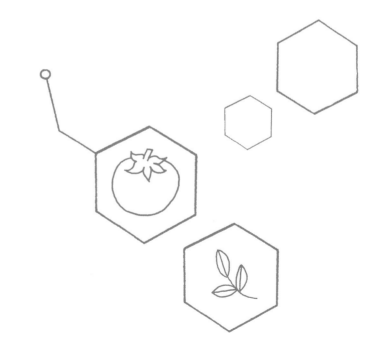

Healthy
HERDS

Now that we've talked about crops, let's move to the other end of the farm: the barn. Can gene editing be used to change animals so they're better suited for human consumption? To create chickens that lay eggs without allergens? Pigs that make low-fat bacon? Beef that doesn't require a cow at all? The answer—you guessed it—is yes. But the number of different ways food scientists are applying CRISPR to livestock production might surprise you.

▎Animal Welfare

In some cases, gene editing can be used to improve the life of the animal itself. Consider, for example, the dairy cow. Most dairy cows have horns. Cool, right? Not so much. Horns may give a dairy cow street cred, but in the barn they're dangerous—not only to the farmer but to other cows as well. For this reason, most dairy cows are dehorned as calves. This process is expensive for the farmer, and painful and stressful for the cow.

As it turns out, those horns are a trait controlled by a single gene, called the *polled* gene. There are two versions of the *polled* gene: the little *p* version creates horns, and the big *P* version does not. The big *P* is dominant over little *p*, which means that if both are inherited, big *P* wins out (see "How's It inherited?," page 28). In beef cows, the big *P* version of the *polled* gene is common (meaning fewer horns), but in dairy cows, little *p* is more common (meaning more horns).

If a cow inherits one copy of the big *P* gene, it will not develop horns.

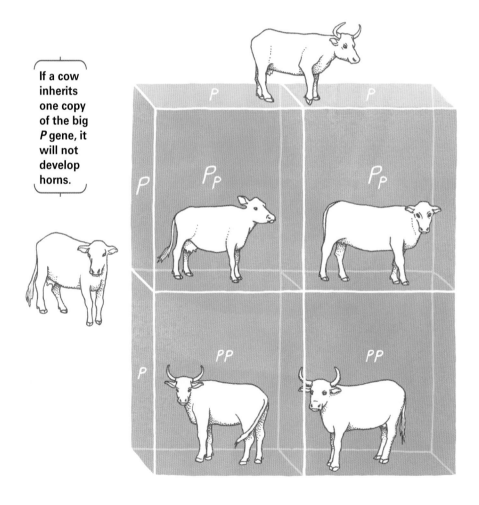

Using dairy cow germ cells (see "Pass It On," page 32) or embryos, scientists have used gene editing with other nucleases (see page 80) to replace the little *p* version of the gene with a big *P* version. The result? A generation of cows born without horns who've passed the trait on to their offspring. No more horns? No more painful dehorning or farming injuries.

With this success, CRISPR is now being considered for similar applications—like gene-edited pigs that are born without tails. As with hornless dairy cows, tailless pigs could be a step forward for animal welfare, since pig's tails are standardly clipped off right after birth (ouch!) so other pigs won't bite them.

Another possible CRISPR application? Since farmers tend to prefer female animals to males (or vice versa, depending on the situation), CRISPR could also be used to limit the number of "wrong sexed" animals that are either killed after birth or castrated. For example, it could be used to help:

- **egg farmers end up with more female chicks (since roosters don't lay eggs)**
- **beef ranchers end up with more male calves (since bulls produce more meat)**
- **dairy farmers end up with female calves (since bulls don't give milk)**
- **pig farmers end up with more female piglets (since pork takes on an odd smell when male piglets go through puberty)**

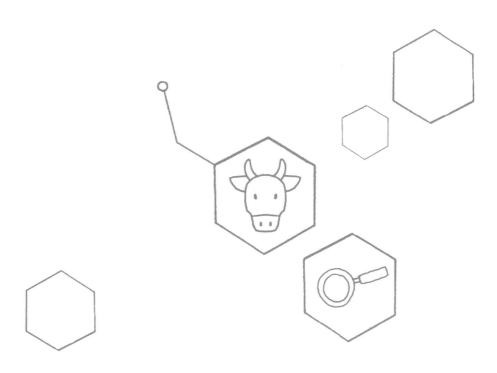

▌ Better Beef

Clearly, gene editing can be used to make sure livestock don't needlessly suffer, but it can also be helpful when it comes to ensuring that the meat, poultry, or eggs are as good as they can be.

Just like some cows have horns and others don't, some cattle breeds have more muscle than others. The variation is partly related to the *MSTN* gene. Myostatin, the protein produced by this gene, stops muscle cells from dividing—a process that inhibits muscle growth in cattle, dogs, and even humans.

Two popular cattle breeds—Belgian Blue and Piedmontese—have 20 percent more muscle than other breeds, thanks to variations in their *myostatin* gene. For ranchers, more muscle means more meat, which has led researchers to study whether CRISPR can be used to knock out the *MSTN* gene in other cattle breeds so they can be as brawny as the Belgian Blue.

Why don't we save ourselves the trouble of editing the *MSTN* gene and just get all our meat from Belgian Blues? Turns out there are other things to consider when deciding what kinds of cows to host on your ranch. Angus cattle, for example, don't do well in hot climates. When the temperature goes up, they stop eating— not a good thing for those who enjoy a beefy steak.

Since Zebu cattle are more suited to a tropical lifestyle, Brazilian ranchers raise them instead. Problem is, Zebu cows produce meat that's tough to chew and not nearly as good as an Angus steak. For this reason, scientists are also working on producing gene-edited Angus cows that can literally beat the heat.

Cows raised in hotter climates are more prone to another challenge as well: disease. As with crops, livestock have been genetically edited to be more resistant to infection. So far, this research has focused on the development of tuberculosis-resistant cattle, avian flu–resistant chickens (see "Animals Get the Flu Too," page 83), and African swine fever–resistant pigs. Since we lose about 20 percent of animal protein globally to disease each year, CRISPR could be a huge triumph for animal breeders, who would also save money on vaccines and medications.

Animals Get the Flu Too

Not only do animals get the flu—they get the same flu we do (try saying that three times fast). Type A influenza viruses can cause avian (or bird) flu, swine (or pig) flu, and a severe version of the human flu complete with sore throat, runny nose, fever, and fatigue.

In wild birds, avian flu doesn't usually cause symptoms. But wild birds can transmit the virus to farm-raised birds like chickens, ducks, and turkeys where it can spread super-quick. This is a big problem. Unlike wild birds, farm-raised birds can get very sick from avian flu. And the only way to stop an outbreak once it's started is to kill the birds—whether they're affected or not.

Although the first reported case of avian flu dates back to 1878 in Italy, outbreaks are on the rise. This is partly due to modern agricultural practices and partly due to the emergence of new viral strains (when a virus mutates, it creates a new version of itself or a new "strain").

During an outbreak in the United States in 2015, an estimated 49.5 million chickens and turkeys were destroyed over a one-month period at an estimated cost of $3.3 billion to farmers, egg and poultry wholesalers, and food service firms. As many birds lost their lives, many people lost their livelihoods. Fear of future outbreaks has prompted a lot of research into finding both a prevention and cure for avian flu—CRISPR included.

In addition to cows, other animals have had their *myostatin* gene knocked out, including lab mice (for research purposes); farm animals such as sheep, pigs, and goats (all in hopes of bringing better meat to the table); and dogs (see chapter 8).

STOP

There are easier (and safer) ways to improve livestock.

Instead of burning off horns or clipping off tails—or genetically editing the animal that carries either trait—we could just give cows and pigs more space. It's only when they're confined that natural traits like horns and tails become a problem.

Besides, once we start talking about editing animals, we're back on that slippery slope. If we keep adding and subtracting traits to suit our dietary requirements, will we eventually edit livestock so much that they no longer resemble the original animals?

And once this technology is available, who's going to limit CRISPR to livestock? If we can create a cow without horns, that means we can also add a horn to, say, the center of a horse's forehead. And while we're at it, we can edit the pigment genes to make that horse white—and market our creation as a unicorn. Or maybe we'll edit a dog so two copies of the little *p polled* gene are inserted and both copies of the *MSTN* gene are knocked out. A hefty horned dog could make its owner a lot of money in an illegal fighting ring . . .

It's even possible to bypass the animal completely and grow meat instead.

While some scientists are focusing on building a better cow (or pig or chicken), others are pushing forward with an entirely different and groundbreaking product: cell-based meat. Also referred to as lab-grown meat, test-tube meat, cultured meat, or clean meat, it's grown by cell culture rather than inside an animal.

Here's how it works:

1. **A sesame seed–sized piece of tissue (containing millions of cells) is taken from an animal.**
2. **The cells are provided with everything they need to grow and divide into muscle: warmth, oxygen, and a nutrient-rich growth medium filled with sugars, salts, and proteins.**
3. **Once the cells have grown to a suitable size, they can be made into hamburger patties, sausages, or chicken nuggets.**

Producing meat this way is clearly better for animals, but it's also better for human health since lab-grown meat never comes into contact with bacteria like *E. coli* or *Salmonella* that can cause disease. Some estimates suggest that cell-based meat requires 99 percent less land, 95 percent less water, and up to 50 percent less energy than traditional meat production—which makes it good for the environment too.

A lot of people, including billionaire Bill Gates of Microsoft fame, have invested in a company that aims to use CRISPR to increase the quality of cell growth in lab-grown meat. While they haven't openly discussed the actual science behind the plan, they have applied for patents to protect CRISPR technology that could allow chicken and cow cells to replicate indefinitely.

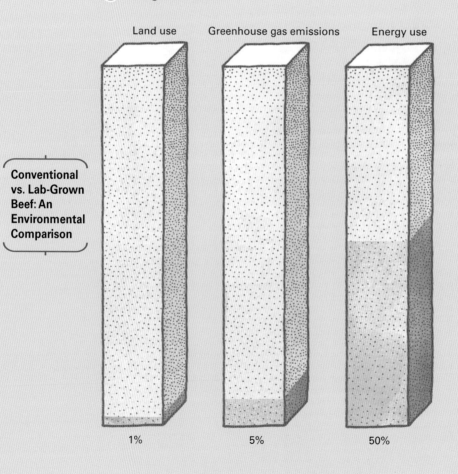

○ Conventionally farmed beef

● Lab-grown beef

Land use

Greenhouse gas emissions

Energy use

Conventional vs. Lab-Grown Beef: An Environmental Comparison

1%

5%

50%

Is the world ready for lab-grown meat?

The first lab-grown hamburger cost $325,000 and took two years to make (we're not talking about a quick trip to your favorite fast-food outlet here!). This is because the growth medium required to feed the cells was very expensive. It was also harvested from unborn calves—obviously not a good thing for those favoring cell-based meat for animal welfare reasons.

But it's possible that CRISPR could provide a solution. The cost of producing cell-based meat has already dropped from six figures to two, thanks in part to gene-edited microbes being put to work making nutrients for the growth medium (just like they've been used to make human medications and supplements for decades). And since the better the growth medium, the better the beef, gene editing also promises to make cell-based meat a lot more tasty.

The real question is: Will people eat it?

Just like with plant GMOs, people are pretty nervous about digging into genetically engineered animals. When the first transgenic animal was approved for consumption—a breed of Atlantic salmon with a growth hormone gene from Chinook salmon inserted into its genome—many people said they wouldn't eat it, and many grocery stores refused to stock it.

Whether people will prefer lab-grown meat over meat from a gene-edited animal over meat from a transgenic animal remains to be seen. But one thing's for sure: the billion-dollar beef industry is going to like gene-edited meat *a lot* more than test-tube meat. How much pressure will they put on the regulators who will ultimately decide whether any of these products are brought to market?

At some point, regulators, farmers, and consumers may not have any choice. Supplying our growing population with enough affordable animal protein may eventually be impossible using conventional farming—whether the animals are gene edited or not.

CUTTING QUESTIONS

A WORTHWHILE INVESTMENT?

CRISPR may be cheaper and easier than previous forms of genetic engineering, but gene-edited livestock still come with a hefty price tag. Some people think it's a worthwhile investment. They believe CRISPR has the potential to make meat more affordable and easier for people in developing countries to produce.

Others think the money would be better spent ensuring the meat we already produce is distributed more evenly around the world. We could get a bigger bang for our buck by addressing the root causes of poverty, supporting farmers in developing nations, and promoting a more plant-based diet.

What do you think? How do you think the money should be spent?

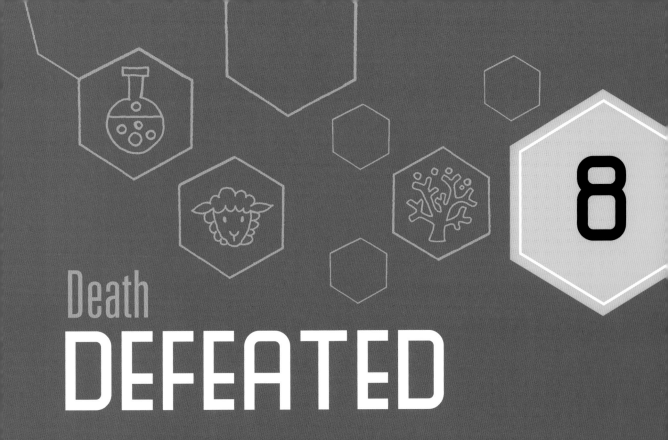

Death
DEFEATED

Okay, so genetically editing a horse into a unicorn is (hopefully) a little far-fetched. But CRISPR applications that can have an impact on our favorite animal-kingdom friends? That's reality. Whether we're talking about building a better pooch, making sure an endangered species doesn't become extinct, or potentially bringing back one that already has, CRISPR is already part of the conversation.

▌Pet Projects

Remember the *myostatin* gene we talked about in the last chapter—the one that stops muscle cells from dividing and prevents certain cattle breeds from getting bulky enough to produce great beef? Well, Hercules and Tiangou are living proof that CRISPR can knock out that same gene in dogs. These two beagles have twice as much muscle as is typical for their breed, making them stronger and faster—qualities that could make Hercules and Tiangou (and their descendants) better police, military, or hunting dogs.

Besides the project with Hercules and Tiangou, CRISPR has mostly been used in dogs to create animal models to study human diseases such as Duchenne muscular dystrophy (a single-gene disorder we discussed in chapter 3). But it's easy to see how this research could also be used to help pets live longer. For example, half of all Cavalier King Charles spaniels die by the age of 10 from mitral valve disease—a condition caused by one of the heart's valves being too narrow. Could this be prevented by knocking out the gene that makes a protein known to mess up heart valves in mice?

Even though there's no single gene (or even group of genes) that CRISPR-Cas9 can edit to make your pet live forever, there are single genes that could be edited to make your pet live longer. And given how many people are willing to pay top dollar to have their animal companions cloned, there's almost certainly a market for this.

> **Hercules and Tiangou have twice as much muscle as the average beagle.**

Speaking of markets, did you know you can buy a micropig for approximately $1,500? Produced by editing a growth-factor gene, a fully grown adult micropig could be about the same size as a medium-sized dog. Originally created to help farmers, because a big pig can be difficult to handle, the micropig has become so popular that the company that created it is planning to sell them in a selection of colors and patterns. Could designer, pink polka-dot, purse-sized pigs be the next big fashion statement to hit the runways?

If you can imagine it, it's probably possible. From modifying man's best friend to editing Komodo dragons into winged dragons, CRISPR could change the way we define our furry (or not-so-furry) friends. (But no amount of gene editing can overcome the physics that prevent an animal from actually breathing fire. Sorry, dragon lovers!)

▌De-extinction

If we can genetically engineer dragons, why not dinosaurs? With CRISPR, the premise behind the wildly popular *Jurassic Park* movies is actually not too far off. While dino DNA's double helix could not have survived fossilization, we do have access to woolly mammoth DNA that's been preserved in ice for thousands of years.

Efforts to clone the woolly mammoth have failed because this frozen DNA is not intact enough to recreate the entire genome. However, scientists have managed to identify the specific genes that made the woolly mammoth different from the modern elephant. These are mostly genes that helped the creature survive cold temperatures, giving them their trademark shaggy coat, sumo-wrestler-sized rolls of body fat, and specialized hemoglobin that kept blood flowing to the most important parts of the body even when the thermostat dipped way down.

Using this information, scientists have modified current cloning techniques to come up with a step-by-step guide on how we could bring the woolly mammoth back from the dead. Here's how it works:

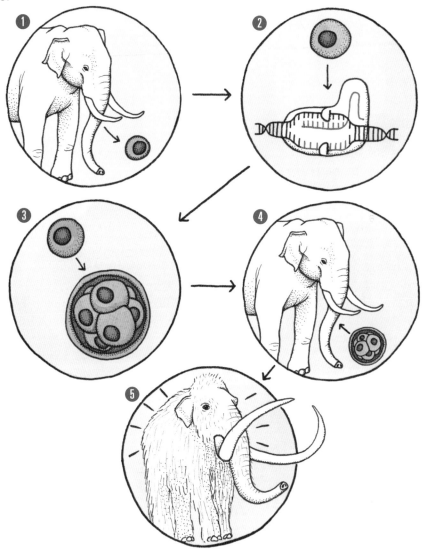

1 Take a cell from an Asian elephant (the woolly mammoth's closest living relative).

2 Unleash the power of CRISPR-Cas9 to edit all 1,642 genes that differ between the Asian elephant and the woolly mammoth (no less than 1.5 million base pairs).

3 Turn the edited cell into an embryo.

4 Implant the embryo into the uterus of an Asian elephant or an artificial womb.

5 And just like that—a woolly mammoth!

The Mammoth Steppe

Let's step away from all this cutting-edge technology and go back, way back (approximately 100,000 years back) to the beginning of the most recent ice age. Along with saber-toothed tigers, cave lions, wolves, bears, bison, reindeer, wild horses, and woolly rhinos, the woolly mammoth roamed the Mammoth Steppe: land that stretched from current-day Spain across Eurasia and the Bering Strait all the way to Canada.

Research suggests the climate was cold and dry, and the land was covered in grasses, herbs, and willow shrubs. Woolly mammoths trampled down little trees as they grazed on the grass, fertilizing the ground with their nutritious dung (yes, dung can be nutritious—to the earth anyway; that's the magic of compost!).

Most woolly mammoths died out after their native glaciers melted 10,000 years ago, but a small population managed to survive in Siberia until approximately 3,700 years ago. This is where scientists have collected mammoth DNA—from the bodies that became encased in permafrost, protecting them from decomposition and hungry predators and scavengers.

What's left of the Mammoth Steppe is now a scraggy, mossy tundra, with areas of ground called permafrost that have been frozen since the last ice age. Tons of carbon from dead plant matter is locked away in the permafrost, which will be released as greenhouse gases when the ground thaws.

But there's some evidence to suggest that woolly mammoths could return this carbon-rich soil to its previous state, preventing the release of greenhouse gases as the permafrost melts. It's one possible justification for bringing the creatures back from the dead.

As for the saber-toothed tiger? Probably best to leave that beast alone.

While there's no proof—yet—that a CRISPR-edited clone could establish an actual pregnancy, scientists are working hard to make it happen. The question is: How much would such an animal actually resemble a woolly mammoth? Not only are the genetics a big question mark, but there's also the very real possibility that Mama Elephant could nurture her baby into being more elephant than mammoth.

Still, the technology might work to develop a cold-resistant elephant (or a so-called mammophant). And what we learn from the elephant-mammoth hybrid could help us resurrect other long-lost creatures.

Woolly rhino

Passenger pigeon

Dodo

Gastric frog brooding frog

Moa

Carolina parakeet

Pyrenean ibex

Thylacine

Invasive Species

As bad as their name makes them sound, an invasive species is any living organism that causes harm when introduced to a new habitat. Sometimes they wreak havoc on the ecosystem; other times they become a threat to human health.

The Asian carp was originally brought to the southern United States in the 1960s and '70s to help keep farm ponds and sewage lagoons free from algae blooms (their favorite snack). Flooding allowed the carp to escape into the Mississippi River System. From there, they spread throughout the states and into the Great Lakes.

● Places where grass carp, a type of Asian carp, have been located.

The big problem with Asian carp is that, well, they're big (especially the bighead variety) and they reproduce like, well, fish (a female can produce up to a million eggs a year). All of this comes with a big appetite. Their aggressive feeding habits can lead to erosion of riverbanks, increased water turbidity, destruction of fish spawning grounds, swings in water temperature, and loss of fish habitat. In addition to stealing food from other fish and aquatic birds such as ducks, they take important nutrients out of the water, killing off sensitive organisms like native freshwater mussels.

Zebra mussels, on the other hand, are an invasive species in their own right. Originally from the Black Sea, they were introduced to the same North American waters as the Asian carp. They form large colonies that cover docks, boats, breakwalls, and beaches, sometimes clogging water intake areas in power stations and water treatment plants. Like the Asian carp, they take nutrients from the water, which impacts the entire ecosystem.

In both cases, scientists are looking to CRISPR gene drives for solutions. Other candidates for the CRISPR chopping block include unwelcome rodents, weasels, and possums in New Zealand and rats in the Galápagos Islands. If you've got a pest, CRISPR may (one day) solve your problem.

There are good reasons to move forward with CRISPR applications in the animal world.

Gene editing could, for example, be more humane than selective breeding and crossbreeding. In chapter 6, we talked about using these breeding techniques in plants, but they're also used in the animal world. Selective breeding, for example, has given the wolf descendants as diverse as the Chihuahua and the Great Dane. And some of our favorite dog breeds are the result of strategic crossbreeding efforts between totally different parents.

The main difference between selective breeding and gene editing is that breeding takes many generations and often requires animals to be kept in captivity much longer. In addition, inbreeding—mating between closely related individuals to promote desirable traits—leads to a lack of genetic diversity that can increase the risk of single-gene disorders such as canine hip dysplasia and complex diseases such as cancer, heart disease, immune disorders, and neurological diseases. For this reason, some people believe that gene-editing pets would be a huge improvement over traditional methods of animal breeding.

Still, personalizing pets or bringing an extinct species back to life through gene editing is a time-consuming and resource-gobbling prospect. Wouldn't all of that effort be better spent preserving the creatures we still have? Turns out CRISPR could help out with that too.

The schnoodle is a cross between a schnauzer and a poodle.

Gene editing can be used to conserve animals—and their environments—in several different ways. To save the Great Barrier Reef, for example, scientists are using CRISPR to determine which genes are vital to the coral reef's life cycle. They're also looking at genes involved in coral bleaching—a side effect of warming ocean waters that "wash out" the algae and starve the reef of vital nutrition.

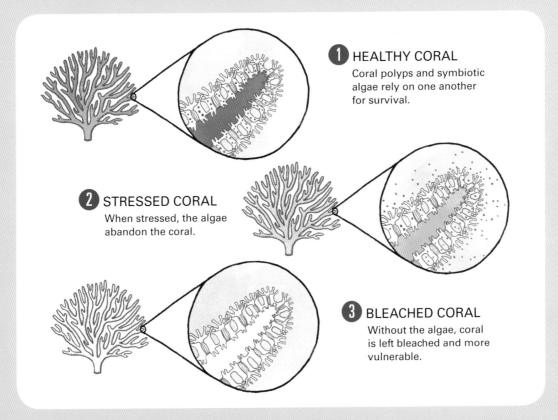

1 HEALTHY CORAL
Coral polyps and symbiotic algae rely on one another for survival.

2 STRESSED CORAL
When stressed, the algae abandon the coral.

3 BLEACHED CORAL
Without the algae, coral is left bleached and more vulnerable.

Another way to prevent extinction is to remove invasive species from native habitats. In what could be considered an "intentional extinction," Asian carp gene drives (see "Invasive Species," page 95) are being considered as a way to eradicate them from the Great Lakes. Ever since this large fish hitched a ride into North America, it's been devastating wild fish stocks. Millions of dollars have been spent trying to control Asian carp through electric barriers, water guns, and scent-based lures.

If we use CRISPR to edit the Asian carp's genome so that the fish produces only male offspring, the species would go extinct from the Great Lakes pretty darn fast. And if that worked, the same technique could be used to deal with other invasive species around the world ("Invasive Species," page 95).

What happens if a gene-edited animal becomes an invasive species?

What if one of those "edited" carp make it back home to Asia, for example? Or mates with a species natural to the Great Lakes? When we're talking about the ecosystem, we have to remember that everything's connected. Sometimes in ways we don't—or can't—predict. If you release a domesticated pet into the wild, for example, it can spread disease to wild animals, steal food from wild animals, mate with wild animals, and generally disrupt the entire web of life (who knew that cute little bunny rabbit could do so much damage?).

Which brings us back to the woolly mammoth. How would these revived creatures fit into the modern world? Would they take food, land, and other resources away from Arctic animals already at risk of their own extinction? Could they become the next invasive species?

Or would they be able to adapt to life at all in today's version of Siberia? We've all heard stories about the person who falls into a coma, wakes up 50 years later, and doesn't know how to deal with anything from microwaves to smartphones. Elephants are smart, social animals that pass down information (such as where to find water in the winter) through learning rather than genetics. Without a woolly mammoth mama, how's a baby going to learn how to survive in the wild? In a world it doesn't even recognize?

As with everything on the slippery slope of gene editing, deciding how to apply CRISPR to de-extinction needs to be done on a case-by-case—or creature-by-creature—basis. And right now, we have no agreed-upon way of making those decisions. Or a crystal ball.

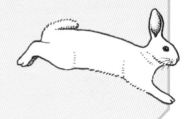

Whether gene-edited animals are ready for the world is one question. Another is whether the world is ready for them.

Gene editing may make a pet pig more manageable (and adorably cuddly) in terms of size, but it might not get rid of the pig's natural instinct to root and dig—a definite drawback if you're living in an apartment or a house with a small landscaped yard.

And what if we extend the lives of dogs or cats to the point where they start outliving their owners? We could end up with more pets in shelters or, even worse, being euthanized. Also, it's too early to say whether micropigs (or any other genetically edited animal) will have additional medical problems, but it's certainly a possibility. In fact, changing a few characteristics of an animal could lead to diseases that are similar—or even worse—than those caused by current breeding techniques.

Finally, what happens if these experiments fail? It's one thing to accept animal testing for the sake of improving human health. But how do we justify hurting animals to create something we can fit in a purse or visit at the zoo?

Animal rights groups have spoken out against cloning, describing it as unethical because it requires animals to be caged and manipulated for no reason other than financial gain. Whether you agree or not, this much is clear: the de-extinction of woolly mammoths will require help from the Asian elephant—a species whose numbers have already been cut in half over the last century due to poaching and habitat loss.

In addition to turning elephants into laboratory specimens for the collection of cells, we have no way of knowing whether an elephant surrogate would actually survive the pregnancy. If she did, what would be the risks associated with going to term and delivering a live-born calf?

In the best-case scenario, where the mammoth calf is born and the elephant survives, there are still no guarantees. Previous efforts to clone animals have shown that clones (especially those born to another species) may be at increased risk for a variety of medical issues.

Through further research, we may be able to solve these potential problems. But questions remain: Is there a reason to bring animals back from the dead or personalize our pets that goes beyond making money? Or satisfying our person-centered desires? Or even making up for past wrongs? It could be that it's best to avoid altering nature any more than we already have.

CUTTING QUESTIONS

A MAMMOTH DEBATE

George Church, the CRISPR pioneer and lead researcher behind efforts to bring back the woolly mammoth, has visions of the majestic creature—or a creature like it—roaming Arctic reserves. He's suggested that, rather than further endangering the Asian elephant, editing their genome to be more "mammoth-like" could actually preserve the species by allowing them to adjust to different climates and expand their habitat. He also believes that bringing back the woolly mammoth could help combat climate change because "they keep the tundra from thawing by punching through snow and allowing cold air to come in." Some scientists agree with evidence that supports this claim (see "The Mammoth Steppe," page 93).

People opposed to bringing back the woolly mammoth aren't convinced. They argue that de-extinction won't make up for past wrongs or clean up the damage we've done to our environment. Reintroducing woolly mammoths to the same world that made them extinct in the first place may, in fact, be unethical. Human activity that may have contributed to wiping them out—such as hunting and habitat destruction—still exists. Some are concerned that mammoth tusks and woolly-skin rugs could suddenly hit the black market and that humans would be no better at protecting the creatures than we were the first time.

What do you think? Should we use CRISPR to bring back a species like the woolly mammoth?

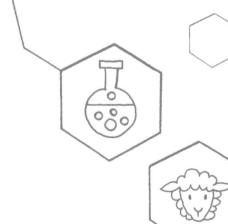

Enhanced
HUMANS

Of all CRISPR's potential power, this application is the one that gets the most attention. When we start thinking about making ourselves better, it's easy to get excited. Who doesn't want to run faster or jump higher (without spending hours pumping weights in the gym)? Who doesn't want to do better on their next math test or English essay (without having to hit the books)? But can we actually create a superior human race through gene editing? The answer is both yes and no.

Better Bodies

If we can use CRISPR to cure a single-gene disorder like sickle cell anemia, we can also use it to create single-gene enhancements like improved memory or extra muscle mass. But things become much more complicated when we start talking about complex traits like longevity and intelligence. Why? Because like cancer or heart disease, there are a lot of genes and environmental factors involved.

With our current knowledge, we aren't even close to being able to do some of the things that show up on news headlines and in social media. Let's take an idea like creating humans with fish tails as an example. Why is this unlikely to happen anytime soon? Because getting a tail to grow requires multiple genes to be turned on and off at different points during the development of specific cells. And we can't do that yet—with or without CRISPR's help.

But if you're eager to give yourself an advantage in the swimming pool, there may be another option: webbed toes—also known as "syndactyly." Syndactyly is actually pretty common; approximately 1 in 2,000 people are born with some version of it because the skin didn't separate during fetal development. While there are several different genes involved in the separation process, it's possible that only one of them needs to be knocked out to significantly increase the chance of developing webbed toes.

Eugenics

During World War II, Nazi scientists and politicians in Germany developed eugenic policies to stop what they described as the "degeneration of the human race," which led to ethnic cleansing and mass sterilization. While the Nazis' eugenic beliefs were later discredited (though not in time to save millions of innocent lives), the sterilization of women with intellectual disabilities remained legal in North America and many European countries long after the war ended.

It's scary to think of how CRISPR might've been used in Nazi Germany (and beyond). But even without someone like Hitler around, it's possible that widespread availability of CRISPR could lead to a "gene gap." Think about it this way: if you can afford gene editing (or have health insurance that covers the procedure), you'd be able to improve your genome in ways that less privileged people could not. Over time, this could lead to an even bigger gap between the rich and the poor and produce a society in which things like deafness or obesity are not accepted.

Who's going to decide what traits should be edited out (or in)? Do we really want a world where everyone has blond hair and blue eyes? We already live in a society that values certain qualities more than others and tends to be intolerant toward minorities. How does CRISPR fit into efforts to promote diversity, while at the same time addressing inequality?

As society moves forward with CRISPR, we also move past "old eugenics," which relied on controlling who reproduces and who doesn't, with the goal of improving a specific race or society. "New eugenics" focuses more on editing the individual to be genetically superior, with the potential to create new qualities yet undreamed of. Is that what Hitler would've wanted?

Looking for an advantage on the field instead of in the pool? We could consider using CRISPR to target genes involved in finger formation. Antonio Alfonseca, Major League Baseball's relief pitcher of the year in 2000, may owe his success to a random mutation that gave him six fingers on each hand—something that could be recreated through gene editing.

Webbed toes and extra fingers may increase athleticism. And giving someone a superpower like infrared vision or a heightened sense of smell could lead to other obvious advantages (and perhaps disadvantages—depending on how stinky your running shoes are). Still, we're going to need a lot more information about the human genome, how genes interact, and the effect of environmental factors on human development to truly be able to turn humans into superheroes.

Syndactyly is a condition where two or more digits are fused together.

Complete syndactyly
of two fingers

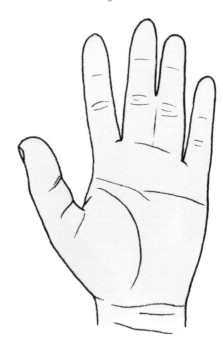

Incomplete syndactyly
of two fingers

◼ Designer Babies

Of course, none of these "enhancements" can be made to a fully grown adult. In fact, they would all need to be made in the pre-baby stage. Which leads us back to the conversation we started in chapter 3 about germline gene editing (see "Pass It On," page 32)—a conversation that really should've started back when the power of CRISPR was reported in 2012. Now, however, it may be too late.

In 2018, CRISPR exploded into the news with the reported birth of "the world's first gene-edited babies." Born in China, the twin girls—Nana and Lulu—were designed to be immune to HIV (see "A Sneak Attack," page 59). He Jiankui, the lead scientist, described the procedure like this:

"[The mother] started her pregnancy by regular IVF [in vitro fertilization], with one difference: right after we sent her husband's sperm into her eggs, we also sent in a little bit of protein and instructions for a gene surgery. When Lulu and Nana were just a single cell, this surgery removed the doorway through which HIV enters to infect people. A few days later, before returning [the embryos] to [the mother's] womb, we checked how the surgery went by whole genome sequencing. The results indicated the surgery worked safely, as intended."

Playing God

A number of international declarations have described human germline modification as both "unethical human experimentation" and an "abuse of human rights." They want it banned—not temporarily, but completely—because they believe it has the potential to change the way we define ourselves as human beings.

According to Charles Darwin, evolution does not proceed toward an ideal model of perfection. Instead, it's a gradual process of adapting to a set of circumstances. Nowhere in nature does it say how a gene should function.

Scientists, however, tend to think of people with "broken genes" as needing to be repaired. Using the CRISPR toolbox to "fix" genes ignores the complex ways we interact not only with our environment but also with ourselves and one another. For those who believe in banning germline gene editing, there are just too many questions that can never be answered.

Could we be creating a whole new species of human being by editing our genome in ways that can be inherited? Will we start defining ourselves by our genes the way we currently define ourselves with fashion? What right do people have to decide what genes are "good" and what genes are "bad"? How do we decide what's best for future generations in a world we cannot predict?

If we can't draw a line between disease and enhancement—or predict the consequences of such decisions—it might just be better to stay out of the sandbox.

Even if the report proves true (at the time this book was published, He Jiankui's research had not been verified or published in a scientific journal), we still have no way of knowing whether Nana and Lulu really are the first gene-edited babies. And if they are, will they be the last? With the speed at which this technology is advancing, probably not.

The better question may be this: Now that the "doorway" to gene-edited babies has been opened, how will it be used next? To improve human health? Produce super-athletes? Wipe out specific groups of people (see "Eugenics," page 102) or design human killing machines?

Germline Gene Editing

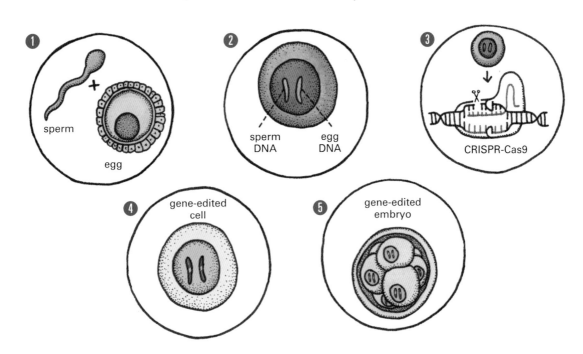

A CRISPR Consensus

Up until now, what's been described as the "CRISPR Revolution" has largely taken place behind laboratory doors or at biotech start-ups and powerful pharmaceutical companies. Policies have been made by some countries, but most discussions have happened among scientists, ethicists, and regulators at prestigious conferences like the International Summit on Human Genome Editing.

It's time—past time, really—to get everyone in the same room to talk about how we want the revolution to proceed. And in today's global climate, we need to make sure every nation is on board with CRISPR rules and regulations—otherwise, we could end up in a new type of arms race to see which country can be the first to use gene editing to its advantage.

Fitting everyone in the world around the same table is difficult, of course, so the World Health Organization (WHO) is attempting to do this work for us. They've put together an international 18-member committee to examine the "scientific, ethical, social and legal challenges associated with human genome editing."

Some advisory committees, such as the National Academy of Sciences (an American nonprofit, nongovernment organization), have already published guidelines for human gene editing that, among other things, restrict germline gene editing to the prevention of a serious disease where there are no other options. But here's where the line gets blurry. Does a condition like sickle cell anemia count as a "serious disease where there are no other options"? There's treatment for sickle cell anemia, as discussed in chapter 3, but it's invasive and expensive and does not provide a cure. How does this compare with making future generations immune to infectious diseases like AIDS and Covid-19?

In addition to trying to answer these questions, the WHO committee is considering a global registry of human gene-editing research. This would help keep everyone up to date on scientific progress, while making decision-makers accountable. It would also allow society to keep track of what heritable changes are being made to the genome so we can follow the consequences of those genome edits over long periods of time.

The next step will be figuring out how to police something like CRISPR, from ensuring that people use the registry to enforcing policy. As we saw with "the world's first gene-edited babies," this will be challenging whether a global consensus is reached or not.

Before we get too carried away, let's take a step back.

Does creating a human being who will never get HIV even count as a "designer baby" enhancement? Opinions on this differ. When we think "designer," we tend to think about something that's upscale or fashionable. But really, the word refers to anything that's planned (usually in a lot of detail) before it's built or made. Still, when we fantasize about the perfect child, we don't often put disease resistance at the top of the list. But it may have been different for the eight couples who voluntarily consented to be part of He Jiankui's study. In all eight reported cases, the father was HIV positive and the mother was HIV negative.

For these couples, having a child who's not only born without HIV but also resistant to developing AIDS for their entire life may indeed be a dream come true.

The controversy surrounding Nana and Lulu has nothing to do with HIV, specifically. It stems from the fact that He Jiankui proceeded without enough proof that using CRISPR to knock out the T-cell's HIV receptor gene in human embryos was safe. In addition to risks associated with off-target changes (see chapter 3) and different delivery methods (see chapter 5), some studies show that people without this receptor may be more susceptible to other infectious diseases such as West Nile virus and the flu.

There's also speculation that it might have an effect on the brain, since lab mice with no HIV receptors are smarter in a way that could translate, in humans, to greater success in school or faster stroke recovery. Even though this could be considered an upside, the point is this: we may not have enough information to decide whether it's ethical to make these types of changes to the human genome, regardless of what gene we're tinkering with. Especially when the edits will be inherited by the next generation, and the next, and the next . . .

If research like this does continue, we must make sure it's part of a properly planned, ethically conducted scientific experiment. It must not become a race to be first out of the gate when it comes to CRISPR-designed babies. And the people involved—the parents and children, not the researchers—must remain top priority.

Are you wondering how He Jiankui got permission to try such a daring experiment in the first place?

He didn't.

Immediately after the announcement was made, the university where he worked stated that they were unaware of the project and put He Jiankui on unpaid leave. Since then, he's been fired and sentenced to three years in prison for conducting illegal medical practice.

Would it have been different if this had happened elsewhere? Hard to say. Policies on both human gene editing and embryo research vary widely. And it's all about the fine print.

In Canada, the United Kingdom, and many European countries, it is illegal to edit the human genome in any way that could be inherited. There are currently no such laws in the United States, but clinical trials involving germline gene editing do not get approved by advisory committees or receive grant funding (which wouldn't have stopped He Jiankui, who reportedly used his own money to fund the procedure). Many CRISPR supply companies also sell gene-editing equipment with a license that restricts its use to non-embryo editing—but they don't necessarily have control over how stuff gets used once it's been shipped.

After news broke about Nana and Lulu, hundreds of Chinese scientists signed a letter saying they were opposed to the research and then posted it on social media. Jennifer Doudna, one of CRISPR's co-founders (see "Who Owns CRISPR?," page 69), went on record saying she was "shocked and disgusted by [the] news" and called on the global scientific community to increase efforts to develop criteria for the clinical use of CRISPR.

This work is ongoing (see "A CRISPR Consensus," page 106), but it's been tough to reach an international agreement on such a controversial subject. In the meantime, many scientists—including CRISPR pioneers

Emmanuelle Charpentier and Feng Zhang—have proposed a temporary moratorium on germline gene editing until there's proof that the technology is safe enough to be used in embryos, eggs, sperm, and the cells that make them.

For some, developing criteria or ensuring the technology is safe doesn't go far enough. Francis Collins, who led the Human Genome Project, called "the world's first gene-edited babies" an "epic scientific misadventure." As director of the National Institutes of Health (part of the U.S. Department of Health and Human Services that decides how over $37 billion in government funding are spent every year on research to prevent, detect, diagnose, and treat disease and disability), he formally stated that the agency "does not support the use of gene-editing technologies in human embryos." In follow-up interviews, he said he had trouble seeing any scenario where germline gene editing makes sense, referring to it as "something that alters the very essence of humanity."

Others believe it will never be morally acceptable to "cross the (germ) line" because it will never be completely safe. No matter how much CRISPR technology improves, scientists will never be sure how much gene editing will change a person overall, especially since it could take decades to see the effects. In addition, the person affected—just a bundle of cells at the time germline gene editing is done—cannot give informed consent: one of the most important requirements for clinical research on human subjects.

No matter how good we get at gene editing, germline changes will remain experimental until we understand all the consequences—which will take many generations to unfold. Beyond this, defining success requires us to make decisions about what it means to be a better human being (see "Playing God," page 104)—a question that gets at the very core of our existence.

As the story of "the world's first gene-edited babies" proves, if the technology is available, people are eventually going to use it.

And if someone's willing to break laws and societal conventions, it can be very hard to stop them.

There are people who think we're making too big a deal out of all this. They compare human germline gene editing to in vitro fertilization, which has gone from a hotly debated procedure to an accepted therapy for infertility.

Have we already crossed the line by helping infertile couples achieve pregnancy? What about when we select embryos for implantation based on whether they have an inherited disease—a practice referred to as "preimplantation genetic diagnosis" (see "Preimplantation Genetic Diagnosis," page 111)? Individuals conceived with this technology do not have a choice, and parents give informed consent for their children to have medical procedures all the time.

Some of the opposition to germline gene editing has more to do with the experimental use of embryos than making heritable changes to the human genome. There are many different opinions on when an embryo becomes a person—based on both religious and moral beliefs—which have led to laws and regulations on how embryos are allowed to be used in research. If we could edit genes in the egg or sperm instead, along with some guarantee that the resulting embryos would be used to create pregnancies (rather than discarded), the debate could change completely. And as with everything CRISPR related, this could soon be possible.

Just as advancements in agriculture have been necessary for our advancement as a species (see chapter 6), advancements in medical technology have allowed people to live longer, healthier lives. Scientists against a moratorium on germline gene editing argue that it will seriously harm innovation. Since CRISPR has the potential to cure disease, what right do we have to stop it?

It's possible that society's ability to use CRISPR to edit our genome is part of our natural human evolution. For some people, the debate boils down to this: If we're smart enough to tinker with our genome—and save lives while we're at it—why wouldn't we?

Preimplantation Genetic Diagnosis

For couples with a single-gene disorder running in their family, preimplantation genetic diagnosis (PGD) is one way to prevent the condition from being passed on to their children. Instead of doing genetic testing after a pregnancy has been achieved, PGD allows genetic testing to be done before an embryo is implanted into the uterus. Here's how it works:

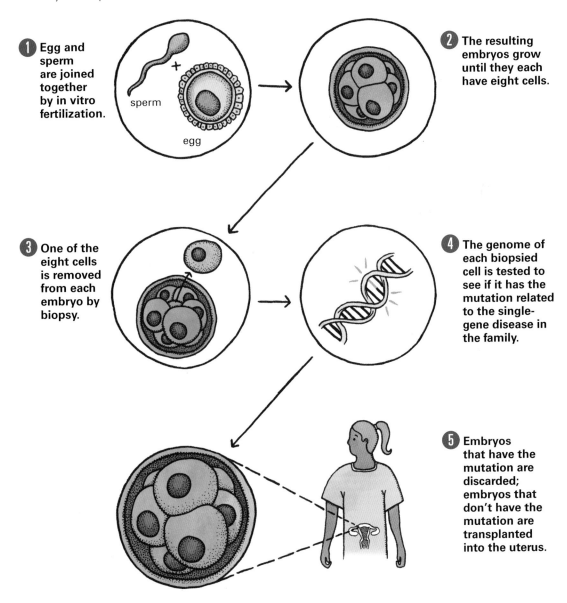

1 Egg and sperm are joined together by in vitro fertilization.

sperm

egg

2 The resulting embryos grow until they each have eight cells.

3 One of the eight cells is removed from each embryo by biopsy.

4 The genome of each biopsied cell is tested to see if it has the mutation related to the single-gene disease in the family.

5 Embryos that have the mutation are discarded; embryos that don't have the mutation are transplanted into the uterus.

Some people are against this procedure because it involves discarding embryos. Other people feel it is a better option than terminating a pregnancy after a genetic test is done at the fetal stage. Either way, it does allow parents to make decisions about what genes get passed on to the next generation—or not.

CUTTING QUESTIONS

PUBLIC OPINION

We've talked a lot about the opinions of scientists, regulatory agencies, and bioethicists. But when it comes to using CRISPR to make heritable changes to the human genome, everyone's opinions matter—including the general public's.

According to a U.S. poll done in 2016, there was a 50/50 split between those who would use gene-editing technology to reduce their baby's risk of disease and those who would not. People were more willing to proceed if there was control over the editing process. They also preferred changes that could make a baby as healthy as the general population (as opposed to "far healthier than any human to date"). Highly religious individuals were more likely to have a moral objection to germline gene editing, especially if it required testing on human embryos.

In a survey done two years later (just before news broke about "the world's first gene-edited babies,"), 71 percent of Americans supported gene editing to protect a baby from an inherited single-gene disorder, and 67 percent supported reducing the risk of complex diseases like cancer. Only 12 percent supported gene editing to improve intelligence or athletic ability, and 10 percent supported altering physical characteristics like eye color or height.

What do you think? Should we use CRISPR to make heritable changes to the human genome?

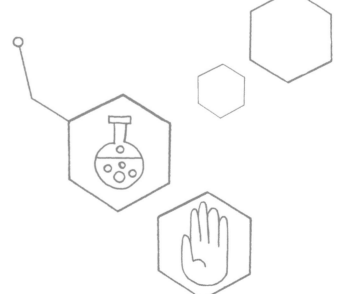

Facing the
FUTURE

CRISPR gives us the power to control the evolution of every species on the planet—including our own. As exciting as the technology is, it isn't entirely new. Before Cas9, there were other more expensive and less powerful gene-editing enzymes. And before gene editing, there was gene modification. So when we wonder "Should we do it?" we're not really asking the right question. Because it's already been done. The right question is "How do we manage it?"

In this book, we've talked a lot about the pros and cons of different CRISPR applications. Now let's take a look into the future and imagine what the world might be like if society decides to "stop," "go," or "yield" on further CRISPR development.

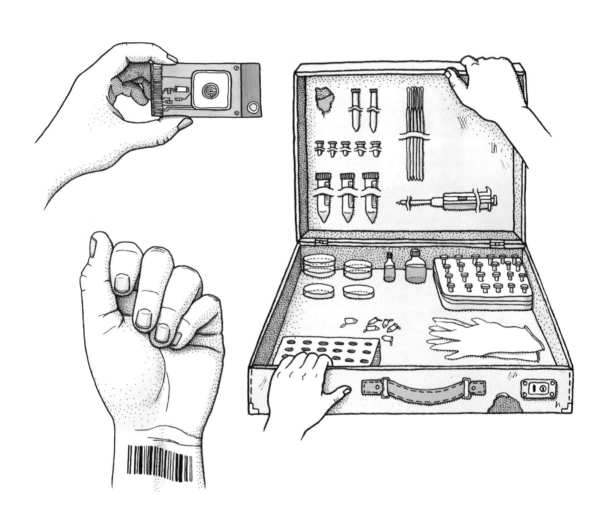

If you even say the word "CRISPR," you'll be fined. Caught with a test tube of Cas9? Jail time.

But that's nothing. Get involved with underground societies trying to use CRISPR to save the world, and you could be executed. All you want to do is buy a DIY CRISPR kit on the black market so you can color your hair without exposing yourself to the cancer-causing chemicals in your mom's hair dye. But even that's risky. And expensive. Because the biohackers are being watched more closely than ever. Just like everyone else.

Now that CRISPR's been discovered, there's no way to "un-discover" it. Putting a stop to gene editing will require consent and cooperation from the entire scientific community. Since this type of universal agreement is unlikely, strict monitoring and enforcement will be required on a global scale.

Stopping CRISPR will also stop—or at least slow—society's efforts to fight disease and provide resources for our growing population in a changing climate. And there's a good chance that those willing to break laws or ignore societal conventions will not use CRISPR for something as simple as hair dye.

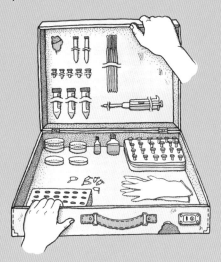

Today's not a good day. You're running late, but you still have to sit at the back of the bus because your barcode tattoo labels you as genetically inferior.

You wish you could switch off the screen in the bus window. It's just showing the same old advertisement that wasn't any good the first time you saw it. If only someone had predicted that using CRISPR to make people smarter would also get rid of creativity. It's been almost 30 years since there was anything worth watching on TV.

With the pace of CRISPR development and the power of its many potential applications, it's a technology that could get out of control really fast. Whether we're talking about enhancing human health or saving extinct species, there are slippery slopes around every corner.

Some gene edits will solve one problem while at the same time creating another. Allowing the market to distinguish between disease and difference, or letting eager investors control gene-drive technology, could have devastating consequences. And it's not something certain parts of society can opt out of, since gene editing affects the entire ecosystem.

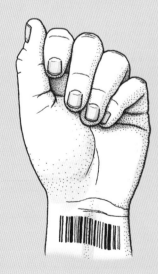

You wake up not feeling great, so you reach for your CRISPR chip.

A quick scan assures you that everything's okay—no new mutations in your genome or evidence of an invading virus or bacteria. For breakfast, you grab a bag of disease-free, drought-resistant, large-eared-corn chips to eat on the way to work. You're part of "CRISPR Cuts," an organization that catalogs genetic edits made to every species on earth so there's a database of changing genomic sequences.

Taking the time and energy to reach a global consensus on how CRISPR will be used, or not used, is vital to its success—and perhaps to our success as a species on this planet. It won't be easy (getting everyone to agree on something never is), but if we can find a way to use this technology responsibly, we'll likely benefit in ways we cannot yet predict.

As with many of society's greatest advancements, no one really knows where CRISPR technology will take us. When cell phones were introduced in the 1980s, no one imagined a future where everyone carries one everywhere, using it for everything from photography to programming (back then, they were expensive and bigger than a brick!). They may have their downsides but smartphones have improved global communication, access to information, and personal safety. Like the cell phone, CRISPR may soon be widely available and capable of improving lives in ways that are beyond our imagination.

But like a discovery such as nuclear energy, CRISPR is also a double-edged sword. When Ernest Rutherford figured out how to split atoms in 1932, he had no idea it would lead to the Cold War and put the world at risk of nuclear warfare. Although nuclear power has reduced the use of fossil fuels to make energy, it's also created nuclear waste and caused nuclear meltdowns. CRISPR could cure disease and help our growing population adapt to a changing climate. At the same time, though, it puts us at risk for the next arms race, eugenics movement, and bioterrorism.

The future may be uncertain, but one thing is clear: CRISPR is here to stay. How we decide to deal with it over the next few years will go a long way toward figuring out what the future might be like.

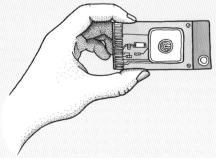

SOURCES

Akst, Jef. "Genetically Engineered Hornless Dairy Calves." *The Scientist*, May 10, 2016. https://www.the-scientist.com/the-nutshell/genetically-engineered-hornless-dairy-calves-33553.

American Society of Hematology. *State of Sickle Cell Disease*. 2016 Report. http://www.scdcoalition.org/pdfs/ASH%20State%20of%20Sickle%20Cell%20Disease%202016%20Report.pdf.

Amoasii, Leonela, John C.W. Hildyard, Hui Li, et al. "Gene Editing Restores Dystrophin Expression in a Canine Model of Duchenne Muscular Dystrophy." *Science* 362, 6410 (October 5, 2018): 86–91. https://science.sciencemag.org/content/362/6410/86.

Begley, Sharon. "After 'CRISPR Babies,' International Medical Leaders Aim to Tighten Genome Editing Guidelines." *STAT*, January 24, 2019. https://www.statnews.com/2019/01/24/crispr-babies-show-need-for-more-specific-rules/.

Biagioni, Alessio, Anna Laurenzana, Francesca Margheri, et al. "Delivery Systems of CRISPR/Cas9-based Cancer Gene Therapy." *Journal of Biological Engineering* 12 (December 18, 2018): 33. https://doi.org/10.1186/s13036-018-0127-2.

Bomgardner, Melody M. "CRISPR: A New Toolbox for Better Crops." *Chemical & Engineering News*, June 12, 2017. https://cen.acs.org/articles/95/i24/CRISPR-new-toolbox-better-crops.html.

Brodwin, Erin. "CRISPR-Edited Food Is Coming to Our Plates and It Won't Be Labelled as GMO." *Science Alert*, April 3, 2018. https://www.sciencealert.com/crispr-gene-editing-tool-food-usda-regulation-gmo-or-not.

Callaway, Ewen. "Controversial CRISPR 'Gene Drives' Tested in Mammals for the First Time." *Nature* 559 (July 6, 2018). https://www.nature.com/articles/d41586-018-05665-1.

Carlson, Daniel F., Cheryl A. Lancto, Bin Zang, et al. "Production of Hornless Dairy Cattle from Genome-edited Cell Lines." *Nature Biotechnology* 34 (May 2016): 479–481. https://doi.org/10.1038/nbt.3560.

Center for Genetics and Society. *Human Germline Modification Summary of National and International Policies*. June 2015. https://www.geneticsandsociety.org/sites/default/files/cgs_global_policies_summary_2015.pdf.

Christian, Jon. "Poll: Two Thirds of Americans Support Human Gene Editing to Cure Disease." *Futurism*, December 29, 2018. https://futurism.com/the-byte/poll-two-thirds-americans-support-human-gene-editing.

Christian, Jon. "Bill Gates Backed Startup Is Using CRISPR to Grow Lab Meat." *Futurism*, March 9, 2019. https://futurism.com/neoscope/bill-gates-startup-crispr-lab-meat.

Cohen, Jon. "An 'Epic Scientific Misadventure': NIH Head Francis Collins Ponders Fallout from CRISPR Baby Study." *Science*, November 30, 2018. https://www.sciencemag.org/news/2018/11/epic-scientific-misadventure-nih-head-francis-collins-ponders-fallout-crispr-baby-study.

Cribbs, A.P., and S.M.W. Perera. "Science and Bioethics of CRISPR-Cas9 Gene Editing: An Analysis Towards Separating Facts and Fiction." *Yale Journal of Biology and Medicine* 90, 4 (December 19, 2017): 625–634.

Cross, Ryan. "CRISPR Is Coming to the Clinic This Year." *Chemical & Engineering News* 96, 2 (January 8, 2018): 18–19. https://cen.acs.org/articles/96/i2/CRISPR-coming-clinic-year.html.

Cyranoski, David. "Super-Muscly Pigs Created by Small Genetic Tweak." *Nature* 523, 7558 (June 30, 2015): 13–14.

Cyranoski, David. "First CRISPR Babies: Six Questions That Remain." *Nature*, November 30, 2018. https://www.nature.com/articles/d41586-018-07607-3.

Delhove, Juliette M.K.M., and Waseem Qasim. "Genome-Edited T Cell Therapies." *Current Stem Cell Reports* 3 (June 2017): 124–136. https://doi.org/10.1007/s40778-017-0077-5.

Doudna, Jennifer A., and Samuel H. Sternberg. *A Crack in Creation: Gene Editing and the Unthinkable Power to Control Evolution*. New York: Houghton Mifflin Harcourt, 2017.

Ehrke-Schulz, Eric, Maren Schiwon, Theo Leitner, et al. "CRISPR/Cas9 Delivery with One Single Adenoviral Vector Devoid of All Viral Genes." *Scientific Reports* 7 (December 7, 2017). https://doi.org/10.1038/s41598-017-17180-w.

Fang, Janet. "Ecology: A World Without Mosquitoes." *Nature* 466 (July 21, 2010): 432–434. https://www.nature.com/news/2010/100721/full/466432a.html.

Ferrua, Francesca, and Alessandro Aiuti. "Twenty-Five Years of Gene Therapy for ADA-SCID: From Bubble Babies to an Approved Drug." *Human Gene Therapy* 28, 11 (November 1, 2017). https://doi.org/10.1089/hum.2017.175.

Finnegan, Gary. "Can CRISPR Feed the World?" *Phys Org*, May 18, 2017. https://phys.org/news/2017-05-crispr-world.html.

Forster, Victoria. "CRISPR in Cancer: Not Quite Ready for Clinical Trials." *Cancer Therapy Advisor*, January 24, 2019. https://www.cancertherapyadvisor.com/lung-cancer/lung-cancer-crispr-not-quite-ready-clinical-trial-use/article/829181/.

Funk, Cary, and Meg Hefferon. "Public Views of Gene Editing for Babies Depend on How It Would Be Used." *Pew Research Center*, July 26, 2018. https://www.pewresearch.org/science/2018/07/26/public-views-of-gene-editing-for-babies-depend-on-how-it-would-be-used/.

Gao, Yuanpeng, Haibo Wu, Yongsheng Wang, et al. "Single Cas9 Nickase Induced Generation of NRAMP1 Knockin Cattle with Reduced Off-target Effects." *Genome Biology* 18, 13 (February 1, 2017). https://genomebiology.biomedcentral.com/articles/10.1186/s13059-016-1144-4.

Gates, Bill. "The Deadliest Animal in the World." *GatesNotes*, April 25, 2014. https://www.gatesnotes.com/Health/Most-Lethal-Animal-Mosquito-Week.

Geib, Claudia. "Companies Are Betting on Lab-Grown Meat, But None Know How to Get You to Eat It." *Futurism*, March 16, 2018. https://futurism.com/companies-lab-grown-meat-none-plans-eat-it.

Gene Watch UK. *GM Mosquitoes in Burkina Faso: A Briefing for the Parties to the Cartagena Protocol on Biosafety*. November 2018. http://www.genewatch.org/uploads/f03c6d66a9b354535738483c1c3d49e4/GM_mosquito_report_WEB.pdf.

Genetics Home Reference. "Cystic Fibrosis." https://ghr.nlm.nih.gov/condition/cystic-fibrosis (accessed February 11, 2020).

Genetics Home Reference. "Sickle Cell Disease." https://ghr.nlm.nih.gov/condition/sickle-cell-disease (accessed February 11, 2020).

Genetics Home Reference. "Huntington Disease." https://ghr.nlm.nih.gov/condition/huntington-disease (accessed February 11, 2020).

Grens, Kerry. "UC Berkeley Team to Be Awarded CRISPR Patent." *The Scientist*, February 11, 2019. https://www.the-scientist.com/news-opinion/uc-berkeley-team-to-be-awarded-crispr-patent-65453.

Hameed, Amir, Syed Shan-e-Ali Zaidi, Sara Shakir, and Shahid Mansoor. "Applications of New Breeding Technologies for Potato Improvement." *Frontiers in Plant Science* 9, 925 (June 29, 2018). https://doi.org/10.3389/fpls.2018.00925.

Hegg, Jens. "Is Intentional Extinction Ever the Right Thing?" *PLOS Blogs*, July 1, 2016. https://blogs.plos.org/blog/2016/07/01/is-intentional-extinction-ever-the-right-thing/.

Howard, Brian Clark. "Invasive Asian Carp Found Breeding in 'Surprising' Location." *National Geographic*, March 12, 2014. https://news.nationalgeographic.com/news/2014/03/140311-asian-carp-upper-mississippi-invasive-species-fish/.

Hsaio, Jennifer. "GMOs and Pesticides: Helpful or Harmful?" Harvard University, August 10, 2015. http://sitn.hms.harvard.edu/flash/2015/gmos-and-pesticides/.

Isakov, Noah. "Future Perspectives for Cancer Therapy Using the CRISPR Genome Editing Technology." *Journal of Clinical & Cellular Immunology* 8, 3 (June 7, 2017). https://doi.org/10.4172/2155-9899.1000e120.

Jacobsen, Rowan. "The Epic Patent Battle That Determined CRISPR's Biggest Winners." *Quartz*, 2019. https://qz.com/1520403/the-epic-patent-battle-that-determined-crisprs-biggest-winners/.

"Gene Knockout Using New CRISPR Tool Makes Mosquitoes Highly Resistant to Malaria Parasite." Johns Hopkins, March 8, 2018. https://www.jhsph.edu/news/news-releases/2018/gene-knockout-using-new-crispr-tool-makes-mosquitoes-highly-resistant-to-malaria-parasite.html.

Karacay, Bahri, "Applications That Make the Cut." *Laboratory News*, February 1, 2019. http://www.labnews.co.uk/article/2024931/applications_that_make_the_cut.

Ledford, Heidi. "CRISPR Deployed to Combat Sickle-cell Anaemia." *Nature* 12 (October 12, 2016). https://www.nature.com/news/crispr-deployed-to-combat-sickle-cell-anaemia-1.20782.

LeMieux, Julianna. "He Jiankui's Germline Editing Ethics Article Retracted by The CRISPR Journal." *Genetic Engineering & Biotechnology News*, February 20, 2019. https://www.genengnews.com/insights/he-jiankuis-germline-editing-ethics-article-retracted-by-the-crispr-journal/.

Licholai, Greg. "CRISPR's Potential and Dangers: Is CRISPR Worth the Risk?" *SciTechDaily*, August 22, 2018. https://scitechdaily.com/crisprs-potential-and-dangers-is-crispr-worth-the-risk/.

Lindsay, Andrew. "Are Genetically Modified Babies Coming Our Way?" *Brainstorm*, February 5, 2019. https://www.rte.ie/eile/brainstorm/2019/0204/1027421-are-genetically-modified-babies-coming-our-way/.

Mann, Paul. "Can Bringing Back Mammoths Help Stop Climate Change?" *Smithsonian Magazine*, May 14, 2018. https://www.smithsonianmag.com/science-nature/can-bringing-back-mammoths-stop-climate-change-180969072/.

Marshall, Michael. "Using CRISPR to Stop Male Calves Being Born May Lower Animal Suffering." *New Scientist*, January 29, 2019. https://www.newscientist.com/article/2192212-using-crispr-to-stop-male-calves-being-born-may-lower-animal-suffering/.

Mendez, Jose, "Cutting Down Malaria with CRISPR: Mosquito Gene Editing as a New Form of Transmission Prevention." *PLOS Research News*, March 12, 2018. http://researchnews.plos.org/2018/03/12/cutting-down-malaria-with-crispr-mosquito-gene-editing-as-a-new-form-of-transmission-prevention/.

McGill University. "'CRISPR Babies': What Does This Mean for Science and Canada?" *Medical Xpress*, January 28, 2019. https://medicalxpress.com/news/2019-01-crispr-babies-science-canada.html.

McKenna, Maryn. "Bird Flu Cost the US $3.3 Billion and Worse Could Be Coming." *National Geographic*, July 15, 2015. https://www.nationalgeographic.com/science/phenomena/2015/07/15/bird-flu-2/.

Mou, Haiwei, Zachary Kennedy, Daniel G. Anderson, et al. "Precision Cancer Mouse Models Through Genome Editing with CRISPR-Cas9." *Genome Medicine* 7, 53 (June 9, 2015). https://doi.org/10.1186/s13073-015-0178-7.

Muscular Dystrophy Association. "Duchenne Muscular Dystrophy." https://www.mda.org (accessed February 11, 2020).

National Academy of Medicine and National Academy of Sciences. *Criteria for Heritable Germline Editing*. https://www.nap.edu/resource/24623/Criteria_for_heritable_germline_editing.pdf.

National Cancer Institute. "CAR T Cells: Engineering Patients' Immune Cells to Treat Their Cancers." https://www.cancer.gov/about-cancer/treatment/research/car-t-cells (accessed July 30, 2019).

National Human Genome Research Institute. "Cloning Fact Sheet." https://www.genome.gov/25020028/cloning-fact-sheet/#al-11 (accessed March 21, 2017).

Nature. "A CRISPR System to Turn Genes On." December 11, 2017. https://www.nature.com/articles/d41586-017-08472-2.

Niiler, Erik. "Why Gene Editing Is the Next Food Revolution." *National Geographic*, August 10, 2018. https://www.nationalgeographic.com/environment/future-of-food/food-technology-gene-editing/.

Normile, Dennis. "Scientist Behind CRISPR Twins Sharply Criticized in Government Probe, Loses Job." *Science*, January 21, 2019. https://www.sciencemag.org/news/2019/01/scientist-behind-crispr-twins-sharply-criticized-government-probe-loses-job.

Nuffield Council on Bioethics. *The Regulatory and Legal Situation of Human Embryo, Gamete and Germ Line Gene Editing Research and Clinical Applications in the People's Republic of China*. May 2017. http://nuffieldbioethics.org/wp-content/uploads/Background-paper-GEHR.pdf.

Osborne, Hannah, "Malaria and CRISPR: Gene Editing Causes Complete Collapse of Mosquito Population in 'Major Breakthrough' for Disease Eradication." *Newsweek*, September 24, 2018. https://www.newsweek.com/malaria-gene-editing-crispr-mosquitoes-1135871.

Oye, Kenneth A., Kevin Esvelt, Evan Appleton, et al. "Regulating Gene Drives." *Science* 345, 6197 (August 8, 2014): 626–628. http://science.sciencemag.org/content/345/6197/626.

Packer, Emily. "Scientists Demonstrate Effective Strategies for Safeguarding CRISPR Gene-drive Experiments." *Phys Org*, January 22, 2019. https://phys.org/news/2019-01-scientists-effective-strategies-safeguarding-crispr.html.

Papadopoulos, Loukia. "World's First Mammal CRISPR/Cas-9 Genetic Inheritance Control Achieved." *Interesting Engineering*, January 26, 2019. https://interestingengineering.com/worlds-first-mammal-crispr-cas-9-genetic-inheritance-control-achieved.

Reardon, Sara. "Welcome to the CRISPR Zoo." *Nature* 531 (March 10, 2016): 160–163. https://www.nature.com/news/welcome-to-the-crispr-zoo-1.19537.

Regalado, Antonio. "First Gene-Edited Dogs Reported in China." *MIT Technology Review*, October 19, 2015. https://www.technologyreview.com/s/542616/first-gene-edited-dogs-reported-in-china/.

Regalado, Antonio. "Top U.S. Intelligence Official Calls Gene Editing a WMD Threat." *MIT Technology Review*, February 9, 2016. https://www.technologyreview.com/s/600774/top-us-intelligence-official-calls-gene-editing-a-wmd-threat/.

Regalado, Antonio. "Farmland Gene Editors Want Cows Without Horns, Pigs Without Tails, and Business Without Regulations." *MIT Technology Review*, March 12, 2018. https://www.technologyreview.com/s/610027/farmland-gene-editors-want-cows-without-horns-pigs-without-tails-and-business-without/.

Regalado, Antonio. "China's CRISPR Twins Might Have Had Their Brains Inadvertently Enhanced." *MIT Technology Review*, February 21, 2019. https://www.technologyreview.com/s/612997/the-crispr-twins-had-their-brains-altered/.

Revill, James. "Could CRISPR Be Used as a Biological Weapon?" *Phys Org*, August 31, 2017. https://phys.org/news/2017-08-crispr-biological-weapon.html.

Saey, Tina Hesman. "In Lab Tests, This Gene Drive Wiped out a Population of Mosquitoes." *ScienceNews*, September 24, 2018. https://www.sciencenews.org/article/lab-tests-gene-drive-wiped-out-population-mosquitoes.

Shapiro, Beth. *How to Clone a Mammoth: The Science of De-Extinction*. Princeton, NJ: Princeton University Press, 2016.

Swetlitz, Ike. "Researchers to Release Genetically Engineered Mosquitoes in Africa for First Time." *Scientific American*, September 5, 2018. https://www.scientificamerican.com/article/researchers-to-release-genetically-engineered-mosquitoes-in-africa-for-first-time/.

Switek, Brian. "How to Resurrect Lost Species: Genetic Experiments Could Bring Back Extinct Animals." *National Geographic*, March 11, 2013. https://news.nationalgeographic.com/news/2013/13/130310-extinct-species-cloning-deextinction-genetics-science/.

Taylor, Ashley P. "Companies Use CRISPR to Improve Crops." *The Scientist*, January 31, 2019. https://www.the-scientist.com/bio-business/companies-use-crispr-to-improve-crops-65362.

Toe, Lea Pare. "Burkina Faso Is Getting Ready for Its Next Stage of Research – Sterile Male Mosquito Release." *Target Malaria*, November 23, 2018. https://targetmalaria.org/burkina-faso-is-getting-ready-for-its-next-stage-of-research-sterile-male-mosquito-release/.

Tontonoz, Matthew. "CRISPR Genome-Editing Tool Takes Cancer Immunotherapy to the Next Level." *Memorial Sloan Kettering Cancer Center*, February 22, 2017. https://www.mskcc.org/blog/crispr-genome-editing-tool-takes-cancer-immunotherapy-next-level.

Ubellacker, Jessalyn. "Buckle Up for Gene Drives of the Future!" Harvard University, June 11, 2018. http://sitn.hms.harvard.edu/flash/2018/buckle-gene-drives-future/.

Wanjek, Christopher. "How Close Are We, Really, to Curing Cancer with CRISPR?" *Live Science*, July 29, 2018. https://www.livescience.com/63192-curing-cancer-crispr.html.

Xia, An-Liang., Qi-Feng He, Jin-Cheng Wang, et al. "Applications and Advances of CRISPR-Cas9 in Cancer Immunotherapy." *Journal of Medical Genetics* 56 (2019): 4–9. http://dx.doi.org/10.1136/jmedgenet-2018-105422.

Yeager, Ashley. "Electric Shock Allows for CRISPR Gene Editing Without a Viral Vector." *The Scientist*, July 12, 2018. https://www.the-scientist.com/news-opinion/electric-shock-allows-for-crispr-gene-editing-without-a-viral-vector-64489.

Zimmer, Carl. *She Has Her Mother's Laugh: The Powers, Perversions, and Potential of Heredity*. New York: Dutton, 2018.

INDEX

FURTHER READING AND MORE INFORMATION

Books

Doudna, Jennifer A., and Samuel H. Sternberg. *A Crack in Creation: Gene Editing and the Unthinkable Power to Control Evolution*. New York: Houghton Mifflin Harcourt, 2017.

Gonick, Larry, and Mark Wheelis. *The Cartoon Guide to Genetics*. New York: HarperResource, 1991.

Metzl, Jamie. *Hacking Darwin: Genetic Engineering and the Future of Humanity*. Naperville, IL: Sourcebooks, 2019.

Zimmer, Carl. *She Has Her Mother's Laugh: The Powers, Perversions, and Potential of Heredity*. New York: Dutton, 2018.

Documentaries

Unnatural Selection (TV series). Directed by Joe Egender and Leeor Kaufman. Netflix, 2019.

Human Nature (film). Directed by Adam Bolt. The Wonder Collaborative, 2020.

TED Talks

Doudna, Jennifer. "How CRISPR lets us edit our DNA." September 2015. https://www.ted.com/talks/jennifer_doudna_how_crispr_lets_us_edit_our_dna.

Henle, Andrea. "How CRISPR lets you edit DNA." January 2019. https://www.ted.com/talks/andrea_m_henle_how_crispr_lets_you_edit_dna.

Jorgensen, Ellen. "What you need to know about CRISPR." June 2016. https://www.ted.com/talks/ellen_jorgensen_what_you_need_to_know_about_crispr.

Websites

The Genetic Literacy Project posts up-to-date articles on human genetics that include links to original or additional sources. Enter CRISPR in the search engine or go to "Human Gene Editing" in the menu at https://geneticliteracyproject.org.

For an overview on CRISPR, including videos, this Vox article is a great place to start: https://www.vox.com/2018/7/23/17594864/crispr-cas9-gene-editing.